THE DAZZLE

BY RICHARD GREENBERG

★

★

DRAMATISTS
PLAY SERVICE
INC.

THE DAZZLE
Copyright © 2003, Richard Greenberg

All Rights Reserved

SPECIAL NOTE

Produced in New York City in 2002 by
Roundabout Theatre Company,
Todd Haimes, Artistic Director.

Originally presented by New York Stage and Film Company
and The Powerhouse Theatre at Vassar in July 2000.

The play is for Peter Frechette,
Reg Rogers, Francie Swift
and David Warren.

AUTHOR'S NOTE

THE DAZZLE is based on the lives of the Collyer brothers, about whom I know almost nothing.

THE DAZZLE was produced by the Roundabout Theatre Company (Todd Haimes, Artistic Director; Ellen Richard, Managing Director; Julia C. Levy, Executive Director) at the Gramercy Theatre in New York City, opening on March 5, 2002. It was directed by David Warren; the set design was by Allen Moyer; the lighting design was by Jeff Croiter; the sound design was by Robert Murphy; the original music was by Lawrence Yurman; the costume design was by Gregory A. Gale; and the production stage manager was Jay Adler. The cast was as follows:

HOMER COLLYER .... Peter Frechette
LANGLEY COLLYER .... Reg Rogers
MILLY ASHMORE .... Francie Swift

CHARACTERS

HOMER COLLYER

LANGLEY COLLYER

MILLY ASHMORE

PLACE

The Collyer mansion in New York City. Bric-a-brac.
Later, impassable mountains of bric-a-brac.

TIME

Early to mid-twentieth century.

THE DAZZLE

ACT ONE

Scene 1

The main room. Stairs to a book-lined mezzanine level. Two pianos. A quantity of stuff strewn about. Lang bursts in, followed by Homer and Milly, all in formal dress.

LANG. I didn't hold the last note long enough!
HOMER. You're mad —
LANG. Not long — not *half* long enough —
MILLY. We didn't hear it that way —
LANG. My foot slipped from the pedal — dead air, all of a sudden, everywhere —
MILLY. However I'm sure you're right —
LANG. *(At one of the pianos.)* I went *(Plays, sings:)* DA DA *DA.*
HOMER. As it was notated in the score; precisely —
MILLY. That doesn't matter —
LANG. And it should have been at *least:* DA DA DAAAAA-AAAAAAAA ... *(Trails the note forever.)*
HOMER. *(After the last vibration dies.)* Well, there, you've made it right.
LANG. There is no making it right —
MILLY. No, how could there be?
LANG. It's not the same thing — it's not the same phrase. Don't you hear? This *(Plays phrase.)* is not the same as *this. (Plays identical phrase identically.)* Don't you hear? This *(Again.)* is not the same

7

as this. *(Again. Beat.)* This *(Again.)* is not the same as this. *(Again. Beat.)* This *(Again.)* is not the same as this. *(Again. Pause.)*

MILLY. *(Thrilled.)* I understand you!

HOMER. Well, you're a great bore who's had an enormous success.

LANG. This *(Again.)* is not the same —

HOMER. Oh, shut up.

MILLY. It was an enormous success, but your dissatisfaction is even more thrilling!

LANG. I didn't hold the note long enough —

HOMER. Langley, on the platform you held the note as long as any of us could stand it; just now, you've held the same note even longer and it's brought us all to the point of complete nervous collapse. Now, please, let us *move on* ...

LANG. It wasn't the same passage, Homer —

HOMER. It was exactly the same passage —

LANG. No, not the same, just *identical.*

HOMER. Ah.

MILLY. Oh.
      Marvelous!
      I love what you've done with this place.

HOMER. Ha-HA!

MILLY. Why do you laugh?

HOMER. Oh, I wasn't, I was hawking.

MILLY. Why are there two pianos, though?

LANG. The other is out of tune.

MILLY. Can't you have it tuned?

LANG. Of *course* not.

HOMER. *(Sitting down to read.)* Can I get you a book, Lang? Something so you can read yourself to sleep?

MILLY. You have a guest here, Mr. — Homer, that is.

HOMER. Oh yes. So sorry, *(Mock cordial.)* Miss Ashmore.

MILLY. Not at all.

HOMER. Can I get you something? Comic book? The Koran?

MILLY. Does one come back to your home, only to be offered books and magazines? Isn't conversation expected; perhaps a cordial or a cigarette?

HOMER. Hard to say, the situation is unprecedented. *(Lang starts to laugh.)* Oh, look, ol' gloomy Gus has cracked a smile —

8

(Langley goes poker-faced.) and off it comes — My brother is *mechant*. Do you know the word *mechant?*

MILLY. I've been to France.

HOMER. Oh yes? Oh really? Oh well, I've been to America yet I don't know the word *(His finger runs down a column in the open pedestal dictionary.)* "meristem." "The unformed growing cellular tissue of the younger part of plants" — well now I *do* know it. However, I suppose France is an older country with a more rudimentary vocabulary. At any *rate:* My brother is *mechant*. He is *insupportable*; he is *incorrigible* —

MILLY. Your brother is an artist.

LANG. *(Quietly.)* Don't say that.

MILLY. And so if he needs to maintain two pianos, one permanently untuned, it should be accepted, unquestioned. We have two pianos, also, but they're on quite separate floors.

LANG. Is one a spinet?

MILLY. Yes …

LANG. And do you — the family — your family, that is — the members of your family, that is — by which I mean the males and the females, that is — do you *group* around the spinet — around the piano *and* the bench, that is — and does one of you play — or do you alternate — or do some combination of you alternate — playing — and the rest of you — or *all* of you, including the one who plays — *sing?*

MILLY. … Yes.

LANG. Or do one — or some of — you — have a wretched voice or wretched voices — and attempt — or attempts — to sing, but fail, or stay silent utterly, or do — all of that — in some — combination?

MILLY. I —

HOMER. Are they songs about poor maidens selling baked potatoes from the curb?

LANG. Homer — please — you're going too *fast* —

HOMER. I merely —

LANG. She hasn't — had a chance — to answer me, yet —

HOMER. All right, Lang —

LANG. I haven't been answered yet —

HOMER. All *right*, Lang —

LANG. Answer me. *(Beat.)*

9

MILLY. *(Brightly.)* Would you mind, terribly, repeating the question?

LANG. *(Sadly.)* I can't.

MILLY. Oh, don't look that way, it makes you ugly, and you were so beautiful tonight —

LANG. No —

MILLY. Yes — you looked dashing …

LANG. Dashing?

MILLY. Yes!

LANG. Did you hear that, Home? I'm dashing!

HOMER. PUH!

MILLY. Am I really not to get a cordial of some kind?

HOMER. Of course. I bid you a cordial adieu.

MILLY. A drink. I'd like a drink

HOMER. Is it that you find rudeness stylish in some way?

MILLY. Yes.

HOMER. And you want to be stylish?

MILLY. Yes.

HOMER. So the more I try to get rid of you, the likelier you are to stay?

MILLY. There must be a bottle of something somewhere. I'm not fussy.

HOMER. Hm. *(Beat. Mock-fancy:)* I believe there's some absinthe in the mud room. *(He rises, goes.)*

MILLY. *(Believing it.)* He likes me so much.

LANG. Oh.

MILLY. What are you looking at?

LANG. A thread.

MILLY. Where?

LANG. In the antimacassar.

MILLY. Which thread?

LANG. That one.

MILLY. The blue one?

LANG. *(Sighs.)* Yes. I suppose that's all we have time to call it.

MILLY. Tell me: What does your brother do?

LANG. … I don't … How do you mean … what do you mean? —

MILLY. His occupation.

LANG. Oh! Oh … He's an admiralty lawyer —

10

MILLY. Really? My, that sounds exciting!

LANG. Yes — the books often have — lovely bindings — retired, now.

MILLY. Retired? So young a man? Why? *(Lang sighs.) That* is a characteristic noise of yours, isn't it?

LANG. What? *(Milly imitates his sigh.)* Yes.

MILLY. Why?

LANG. People ask me questions —

MILLY. People ask everybody questions.

LANG. I don't have wind enough for a single complete answer. That would seem to be the difference.

MILLY. Do you like me?

LANG. ... Yes.

MILLY. That's all the answer I need.

LANG. That was a yes or no question.

MILLY. I'm going to ask you a harder one. What do you like about me? *(Lang sighs.)* More than that. Tell me. I'm not expecting a complete answer. I'd find a complete answer insulting. Tell me a little: What do you like about me?

LANG. I find your money thrilling, and I'm fond of your hair.

MILLY. *(On to him.)* Which hair?

LANG. *(Points.)* That one.

But even that's a group. *(She leans over and kisses him.)*

MILLY. Did you mind my doing that?

LANG. It was all right.

MILLY. Touch my hair.

LANG. *(Baffled for choice.)* U-u-u-h-h ...

MILLY. Start with your favorite ... *(He puts his hand to a ringlet, caresses it.)* That's nice.

It's so strange you like my money. I've always rather detested it myself.

LANG. *(Neutrally.)* That's stupid.

MILLY. Well, I have. It's not mine, yet one day it will be mine, although I've never done anything to earn it —

LANG. It's in something like — tallow — or gypsum — isn't it?

MILLY. Something like.

LANG. Yes — something where there are *fields* — or *mines* or caverns — and laborers go — *out* — to them —

11

MILLY. Ha-ha —

LANG. — and labor in them — and then come back with their *plunder* —

MILLY. Yes, I come from robbers, long lines of robbers, unconscionable —

LANG. — and never — do they — think of the fields whence the plunder comes — do they? —

MILLY. They're horribly exploited —

LANG. But — am I right? Do they — really — just come home — or go to — pubs — and drink beer and eat oysters and *forget*? Is that it?

MILLY. Well, I can hardly be expected to know what goes on in the minds of some grubby workers — but — probably — yes — I mean, they're dumb as posts, for the most part.

LANG. That must be nice. I would like to be one of them.

MILLY. Idiotic idea!

LANG. Why?

MILLY. You could no more be a laborer than I could —

LANG. I didn't say I *could* be, I said I would *like* to be —

MILLY. That sort of thing should revolt you; it's the very opposite of you —

LANG. Those two ideas don't go together — why wouldn't I want to be the opposite of myself? I don't propose my character as an ideology — it's a condition — it's my condition — it wasn't chosen, it wasn't elected by — although you're right, I don't like to sweat. *(Pause. He continues to fondle her curl, staring at it.)* At seven P.M. most nights ...

... at seven P.M. most *week*nights ... I sit in that window — *that* window —

At seven P.M. most weeknights, I will sit in the wing chair in that window and stare through the window, the evening paper propped in my lap, as a sop to the neighbors — who might be — sometimes *are* — have, at any rate, *begun* to — stare back — and I'll watch the men return from business.

Especially this is in late fall, and early winter — coats are important — thick collars turned up — and a current of wind — a light current of wind that seems — this is an illusion — that seems to speed them along.

They are accompanied by leaves. Curled umber and orange and sepia at their feet, sped by the wind — that's *not* an illusion. Lit torchieres in the neighbor's windows — dogs — I'm sorry, I meant to warn you, this is a senti*mental* story — and the men — what I mean is, their lower extremities all, what I'm trying to say is: Their *gait* is terribly relaxed. As they approach their own houses, the day of business behind them, whiskey waiting — I've seen that through the window, that's *not* illusion — roasts of beef — and oh — well — children — and as they walk — stride — almost skip — their marvelous chins goosing butterflies — their wooden sticks and leather bags jaunting forth — it's a kind of unleafing of the day — it borders on the visible how they scatter behind them what's come before — at seven P.M. as they approach their homes — via the River Lethe — ha-ha! — and they will sometimes catch my eye — and nod to me! — as if we are the neighbors that we are — as if what *is* … *is* — as if this is *my* seven P.M., too — a little nod — and I'm swung into the circle of their hour — but then that stops — and the next hour is smashed to smithereens — like my aunt Prudy's cheap lacquered vase — *(Beat.)*

MILLY. I come from swine.

No, I live among the most remarkably unpleasant people.

What time is it? I stay out so late all the time so as not to have to return to Fifth Avenue.

You don't know what a hell it is there!

Oh, it's so lovely your poetry of seven P.M.! But I've spent that same hour cowering in an upstairs room, cowering with the lamp unlit, hiding … hoping for … something … *(She takes his hand, puts it on her breast.)*

LANG. No, I'm not done here yet. *(He puts his hand back on her hair.)*

MILLY. You're a miracle, Lang. *My* miracle. I've lived most of my life in a kind of sleepy terror. With you, I'm afraid but completely awake! I never know what you'll do or what you mean. You disconnect everything.

LANG. Yes. It's like how menacing a man can seem, pausing on the sidewalk at a peculiar angle, until you realize he's walking a very low dog. *(Homer enters carrying bottle and glasses.)*

HOMER. I couldn't find anything.

MILLY. Anything?

HOMER. To drink. *(He places glasses on table, pours one drink.)*

MILLY. Nothing of any kind?

HOMER. *(Pouring.)* No.

MILLY. No beverage of any kind?

HOMER. So terribly sorry. None. *(He swallows, lets out a satisfied breath.)*

MILLY. Well, that's all right. I'm not really thirsty.

HOMER. Langley.

LANG. Yes, Homer.

HOMER. Remove your hand from that lady's coiffure.

LANG. But I almost have a name for its color.

HOMER. No one cares.

LANG. *I* do.

HOMER. That is not sufficient reason to keep it up. Please. *(Langley takes his hand out of her hair. The hand trembles.)* Thank you. *(Pause.)*

MILLY. *(Pours herself a drink.)* How exciting it must have been, Admiralty law, I mean.

HOMER. Why?

MILLY. I think the sea is the most exciting thing! The air, all salt, all brackish, and then the weather vanes and ... nor'easters and whatnot — Isn't it? Didn't you find?

HOMER. Admiralty lawyers do not sail. *(Beat.)*

LANG. You did —

HOMER. What?

LANG. — *stand* on a battleship, once, and have your photograph taken ... didn't you? *(A smile blooms slowly between them.)*

MILLY. Why did you give it up? *(Homer looks at her. He takes the glass from her hand.)*

HOMER. I was needed here.

MILLY. For what reason?

HOMER. *(Crossing to Lang.)* I am my brother's ... *(Hands him glass.)* accountant.

14

Scene 2

Homer storming. Lang playing a lugubriously slow and unrecognizable piece on the piano.

HOMER. You *must* listen! You must take this in, Lang! You cannot keep up this *policy* of *caprice* with your booking agents! Your position is not so secure as all that, you know; your reputation is a little teeter-y — they will drop you, do you understand? Drop you cold if you keep withdrawing like this — at a moment's notice and on the flimsiest of pretexts. "I have a cold in the nose." You don't *play* with your nose — although at this rate that will come next! At least — say — something — like — oh! an andiron fell across my wrist, or some such, and we can make a splint and *show* them something — but it seems to them like actual spite. As if you're playing out some sort of contempt. You cannot do that, Lang. These are agents, managers, functionaries in the world of art, they already suspect themselves of being louts, if you confirm it for them, they'll make you *pay* — which brings me to my *next* point — which is, we have *bills* to pay, and if you think we're bottomlessly rich, let me disabuse you right — do you think when our parents moved to Harlem it represented a *burgeoning* of the family fortune, because — and — oh, yes — this house is *big* — but that's because the neighborhood might as well be Praetoria — as convenient as it is to where — things are really *happening* — you — once you seemed to have some *sense* of — what was what — but with every passing day you become — more and more — less and *less* — sensible, I mean — and, meanwhile, *I'm* left with the paperwork, with the mounting debt, with the task of diplomacy — even in the neighborhood — the butter-and-egg men do not hold us *dear,* really, they could do very nicely without our custom — especially when we're in arrears to them — well, the way you *sniff* the eggs — what are they supposed to think? — really Lang, you have no idea what I go through in the course of a — day — your circumference, I know, is *vast*, but my circuit is intricate

15

— and debilitating — and I'm only asking for you to cooperate —
a little bit — with — IS THIS "THE MINUTE WALTZ"?
LANG. Yes. *(He plays the last note. It lingers forever.)*
HOMER. Oh God, we're doomed.
LANG. Were you speaking to me before?
HOMER. Yes.
LANG. I wasn't listening. *(Beat.)*
HOMER. Ah.
LANG. I was playing.
HOMER. Yes. I heard. It was very impressive. You completed
"The Minute Waltz" in slightly under three quarters of an hour —
LANG. It was quite nice —
HOMER. Next year this time, you'll have to take an intermission.
LANG. Are you *upset?*
HOMER. ... Of course not.
LANG. You are, though. I think you are. Why? Be specific.
HOMER. No reason. No reason at all.
LANG. It doesn't have anything to do with *me*, does it?
HOMER. How could it? *(Pause.)* You need to get things under
control, Lang.
LANG. What things?
HOMER. You need — are you listening to me now?
LANG. Yes —
HOMER. Are you really?
LANG. I'm not playing —
HOMER. All right. You need to — not even in your *head* —
LANG. I promise you, Homer, you are my only music at the
moment.
HOMER. You need to — conduct yourself in a more — well,
don't listen like *that* — please —
LANG. Like what?
HOMER. With such — rapt — concentration —
LANG. Why not?
HOMER. Because, in the first place, I'm not going to say any-
thing delightful. In the second place, there are — there *should* be
— natural modulations to — the art of listening — and, in the
third place — it's just creepy.
LANG. I'm sorry, Homer.

HOMER. That's — fine — look — you have to conduct your business in a more business-like way.

LANG. Ah. *(Beat.)* I don't know what that means.

HOMER. It means — for example — you have to stick to your word.

LANG. I do stick to my word, Homer —

HOMER. Lang —

LANG. Or — well — actually — it's more like my *words* stick to *me* — I mean — I speak in a kind of stream — and usually — I try to do whatever it was I said last.

HOMER. That's not how business is conducted.

LANG. It *ought* to be.

HOMER. But it *can't*. If in September of 1904 you promise to perform Schubert at such-and-such a place in August of 1905, you are expected to perform Schubert at such-and-such a place in August of 1905.

LANG. Well, that's ridiculous.

HOMER. It isn't.

LANG. It *is* and I'm not going to explain why because I just don't have the wind for it, at the moment. You should know, anyway, Homer; you should know why. *(Beat. Homer sits.)*

HOMER. Do you want to be old and sick and hungry and without a home?

LANG. I can't say, I haven't tried.

HOMER. *Would you please care enough about me to* accept *a* premise?

LANG. ... Yes, Homer, I'm sorry.

HOMER. We are not in trouble at the moment —

LANG. Then may I go?

HOMER. But we *may be* shortly.

LANG. ... Hm. Ah. How shortly?

HOMER. I don't — does it matter?

LANG. Yes.

HOMER. ... *Very* shortly.

LANG. "Very." Timid, empty stark little word.

HOMER. Tomorrow, the day after, ten years from now — all I am saying is we have to take *the long view* — *(Lang returns to piano, plays a chord, holds it.)* Lang!

17

LANG. Do you hear that —

HOMER. All Harlem hears that —

LANG. … If that were true …

HOMER. I am so sick of these chords you bang out — at random — night and day — they reverberate endlessly — they've worked their way into the curtains, I swear it, like some old bad stench of cigar smoke or —

LANG. Most smells are actually pleasant if you don't know where they're coming from.

HOMER. *(Slams hands onto piano top.)* Lang!

LANG. … Yes, Homer?

HOMER. What do you think of the girl?

LANG. What girl?

HOMER. Oh Lord — the girl — the girl — the rich girl — who sits beside me at your recitals — and swoons and gasps and sways as though she were the music — what do you think of her?

LANG. Mildred.

HOMER. Yes.

LANG. Milly.

HOMER. Yes.

LANG. Her name is Milly.

HOMER. That does not constitute an opinion.

LANG. Doesn't it?

HOMER. I believe that she's in love with you. *(Pause.)*

LANG. Huh.
   Is that…?
   Really.

HOMER. I believe so.

LANG. What does that mean?
   Tell me exactly.
   Turn on the lamps first.

HOMER. It isn't dark.

LANG. It will be when you finish.

HOMER. I am not going to go … into all that.

LANG. Why not?

HOMER. Because … it isn't definable.

LANG. Then on what authority do you speak of it?

HOMER. One can … *feel* it, without … being able to … put

18

into words —

LANG. I don't agree — I think a word can exist without a meaning but a meaning can't exist without a word — music is better than either, because it forgoes both — that's why I hate books — books always seem to me like music explaining itself under duress. But what were you saying?

HOMER. I don't remember.

LANG. Love! That was it. You were going to define it.

HOMER. I was attempting *not* to —

LANG. Because you've never experienced it? *(Beat.)*

HOMER. You live only to torture me, don't you?

LANG. Not at all.

HOMER. I *have* — experienced —

LANG. Oh poo — *where? When?*

HOMER. Lang —

LANG. When you were away?

HOMER. Yes.

LANG. When you were away in — oh, what is China always called in the disintegrating books — *Cathay?*

HOMER. Among other places.

LANG. Really?

HOMER. Yes.

LANG. Really?

HOMER. Yes!

LANG. Oh, Homer, why must you lie *at home?* Lying is for outdoors — this is our house!

HOMER. I am *not* — I have a very real past —

LANG. There is no such thing —

HOMER. I ... have ... had ... have had ... one.

For all the good it does me now.

I was ... a different person. Before.

You must grant me that, it's my solace.

Oh Christ Christ Christ Christ, why are we — *(Pause. He sits.)* I know you can't answer this next question, but I'll ask it anyway: Do you love her?

LANG. Oh, I can answer that.

HOMER. You can?

LANG. Yes. I know what love is; you're the one who can't define it.

Do I love her?
Yes.
I believe I do.
HOMER. Truly?
LANG. Yes.
I believe so.
There's something ... miasmic about her.
HOMER. Miasmic?
LANG. Yes. It's her speech! It's when she speaks. You see, she has nothing to say; and she says it incessantly. There's never a phrase, a word — an accent, even — that hasn't been thoroughly modified by convention, made virtually inaudible by overuse. She's so ordinary! It's as though ordinariness had been rubbed into the very *nap* of her voice — her voice lulls me! — It has none of the hooks and snares of most voices — why, Homer, she very nearly bores me, and hardly anything does that! I can imagine living with her as one would beside a narrow and uninteresting body of water — scarcely even aware of its existence — yet made utterly tranquil by its flow.
Yes. I love her.
And sex is not a problem for me, you know. I mean, it's no more intense than anything else. *(Pause.)*
HOMER. Well, then ...
LANG. Why do you ask?
HOMER. No reason. *(Beat.)* She's very rich. *(Beat.)* No reason.

Scene 3

Offstage a string quartet plays a waltz. People dance. Light slips in under the doors. The doors burst open: Milly and Lang, laughing. Formal party dress.

MILLY. Oh, what a funny idea!
LANG. What?

MILLY. This! This party here! It's —
LANG. The music is —
MILLY. — in the Collyer Manse — of all places —
LANG. — excruciating —
MILLY. — it's — no — very sweet — a string quartet —
LANG. The cello is flat —
MILLY. — no one minds —
LANG. — a sixty-fourth tone flat —
MILLY. A sixty-*fourth* tone!
LANG. Yes.
MILLY. There is no such thing as a sixty-fourth tone —
LANG. There is.
MILLY. People can't *hear* a sixty-fourth tone.
LANG. Other people.
MILLY. Don't listen.
LANG. I can't help it —
MILLY. *(Kisses him.)* Don't. Why are you having this party?
LANG. It was my brother's —
MILLY. At my family's, by the way, there's an orchestra —
LANG. It was Homer's idea —
MILLY. A full symphony orchestra —
LANG. He thinks we need to woo the neighbors — Christmas!
He thinks like that. He has a holiday mentality. He thinks in great
chunks of time, punctuated by the advent of God.
MILLY. Well, people do.
LANG. He's terribly excited lately — he thinks we're becoming
banal — the prospect exhilarates him!
MILLY. I'm so glad to be here, with you, and not at home with
all the horrible, horrible people. Thank you for inviting me.
LANG. It was Homer's idea.
MILLY. Really.
LANG. It's part of his new life. He's having a new life. It's all very
funny, but we mustn't giggle about it in his presence. Do you like
the neighbors?
MILLY. They seem —
LANG. They don't care for me.
MILLY. I'm sure —
LANG. — and this is an ever — worsening — situation — I

21

think we're in bad credit or something — with some of them —
and that makes the others — gabble — about us — although
Homer, I think, I think Homer is all right — still — beside the
pale, not yet beyond it — isn't it funny? — when they all seem to
me — harrowingly peculiar — but I'm — apparently not — to
judge — *(Homer enters.)*
HOMER. *(To Milly.)* You're not drinking. You must let me get
you something —
MILLY. We're fine —
HOMER. We? Are we speaking the language of "we"?
MILLY. For the evening.
HOMER. Life has become a three-volume novel.
MILLY. Hardly.
HOMER. That's all right — it's what I'd hoped — *it's what I'd
hoped! (He exits.)*
MILLY. Your brother —
LANG. He is —
MILLY. Last year I visited Vienna — they're doing marvelous
things in the mental field — it might behoove him to —
LANG. Oh, please, no.
MILLY. Lang, you might have noticed I have some very modern
ideas —
LANG. No. I never noticed you had *any* ideas.
MILLY. ... Nevertheless.
LANG. That doesn't mean —
MILLY. Nevertheless, I —
LANG. That doesn't mean that you *lack* them —
MILLY. — no — I —
LANG. Only that I don't care about any ones you may have.
MILLY. *My point is ...* I might be a bit much for you to take in
all at once.
LANG. Everything is a bit much for me to take in all at once.
MILLY. I mean ... *I* might be ... in particular.
LANG. Everything is particular. You're a little less so. That's why
I can be with you.
MILLY. ... I don't know how to make out ... what you're saying
to me —
LANG. That can be a problem.

MILLY. You seem to speak entirely in ... strategies ...

LANG. No, you're wrong. I speak in rocks.

MILLY. Rocks?

LANG. Yes. Rocks: My words are not absolutely solid, but near as it gets.

MILLY. But I think sometimes what you say — insults me —

LANG. No, you're wrong. To insult someone is to aim for his feelings — I never aim for people's feelings — I never do anything with people's feelings, I leave them alone, like books.

MILLY. Interesting. *(Re: the music.)* Oh, this one — I love this waltz —

LANG. Yes — it's even nicer in tune —

MILLY. Can we dance?

LANG. I doubt it.

MILLY. *(Opening her arms.)* Lang.

LANG. No. I doubt it.

MILLY. Please try. *(Lang sighs, enters her arms. She leads. She dances in tempo to the music, he only goes half that rate.)* You're dragging the tempo.

LANG. No, I'm perfectly in tempo — it's you and the musicians who're going wrong. *(She tries to speed him, he pulls away, continues dancing, alone, at his rate.)* It's better this way.

MILLY. All right. *(He dances alone. She dances alone, twice as fast.)* This is nice.

LANG. Much nicer.

MILLY. But I miss holding you.

LANG. Hmmm ...

MILLY. And you miss me.

LANG. I do?

MILLY. Yes.

LANG. Oh.

MILLY. The feel of me.

LANG. I miss that?

MILLY. Yes.

LANG. Oh.

MILLY. You miss it severely.

LANG. Really?

MILLY. Yes.

LANG. I didn't know.

MILLY. Well, now you do.

LANG. Thank you. I'm grateful for the information.

MILLY. Lang?

LANG. Yes.

MILLY. You dance divinely.

LANG. Yes. That would be the only explanation.

MILLY. Lang?

LANG. Yes?

MILLY. Your brother, Homer?

LANG. That's not a question; why did your voice go up?

MILLY. Why do you suppose he is to me as he is to me?

LANG. I don't know what you just said.

MILLY. His behavior toward me is positively schizophrenic.

LANG. Lord, that's an interesting word! *(Homer appears on the mezzanine, unseen by them.)*

MILLY. He shuns me, then he courts me — do you suppose there's something in his past — some deep after-trace from his childhood that he sees replicated in me and that he's trying to banish or fix in some way?

LANG. … Hmm?

MILLY. I said —

LANG. Homer is having a tragedy. He's a tragic figure. We are, apparently. If I start to giggle, please excuse me. *(He dances half the tempo again, virtually at a stop. She speeds slightly.)*

MILLY. In what way tragic?

LANG. Oh, I don't know. I don't understand these things. What is tragedy? I wrote it in a notebook once.

MILLY. Tragedy is — a feeling more than any —

LANG. Oh, yes, I remember! Tragedy is when a *few* people sink to the level where *most* people always *are*. That's what happened to him — to us! That's why he's, what, sycophantic —

MILLY. Schizophrenic —

LANG. Polysyllabic. This is all nonsense, though. You make me speak nonsense. It's pleasant.

MILLY. What is the nature of the tragedy?

LANG. Oh — I don't — don't ask that so passionately — as if it was — as if it *was* — financial, I —

MILLY. Financial reversals?

LANG. Homer promises we'll end starving in the gutter. I find that provocative.

MILLY. And now he's suddenly kind to me.

LANG. Is he? Well, good. *(She's paused.)* Why have you stopped dancing? The excruciating music plays on —

MILLY. Lang?

LANG. Another rhetorical question.
Yes. I am.

MILLY. This dress I'm wearing?

LANG. *(In imitation.)* These shoes I've donned?

MILLY. It's very cunningly made.

LANG. Yes.

MILLY. It wraps and wraps.

LANG. I like — the way that happens —

MILLY. — and unwraps — and unwraps —

LANG. Which will make it possible for you to bathe!

MILLY. *(Unwrapping from the top.)* There's a wonderful feel to it — would you like to feel?

LANG. I don't know that — I have the time —

MILLY. It's silk — silk against my skin — did we lock those doors?

LANG. No.

MILLY. No matter. Won't these layers look marvelous on the floor?

LANG. Against the Oriental rug, yes. *(He tries to dance again, stops.)* Yes.

MILLY. Yes. Textures are endlessly fascinating, don't you think?

LANG. I ...

MILLY. Combined. Revealed. *(She is now topless.)* Don't you think?

LANG. God.

MILLY. Lang.

LANG. You are —

MILLY. Lang —

LANG. Such a *fact* — standing there —

MILLY. Do you want to touch? Would you like to touch?

LANG. ... Yes.

MILLY. You may.

LANG. May I.

MILLY. Yes. *(He goes to her, drops to his knees, buries his head in her dress.)*

HOMER. Not the *dress*, idiot, the *girl!*

LANG. Homer!

HOMER. You've misunderstood.

LANG. You should — cover up —

MILLY. That's all right —

HOMER. *(Descending.)* Not on my account —

MILLY. That's all right — I don't mind —

HOMER. No need to cover up on my account —

LANG. We didn't — know you were there —

MILLY. I did —

LANG. — You? —

MILLY. I saw.

HOMER. And you — stripped — anyway?

MILLY. I thought it was what you wanted —

HOMER. What I — ?

MILLY. — wanted —

HOMER. What does that have to do with anything?

MILLY. I thought it was what Lang wanted —

HOMER. What Lang wanted?

MILLY. It was for the greater good of you both. And it was what *I* wanted. *(Beat.)*

HOMER. *Fix* yourself. *(Pause.)*

MILLY. Yes. All right. *(She pulls up the dress; it covers her loosely.)* There. Is that worse?

LANG. Much worse.

MILLY. Hmm.

LANG. Much, much worse. All disappeared.

MILLY. Sit beside me.

LANG. Taken back.

MILLY. Sit beside me, you can hold my dress. *(He sits beside her.)*

HOMER. *(Lights a cigar.)* We are having a grand success tonight, Lang. We are gone from the bottom to the top in the neighbors' estimation. Before they reviled us as scum, and now they resent us as gentry: could there be a more satisfactory —

MILLY. May I have a cigar?

HOMER. No.

Yes, a grand success. Very exciting. We'll be welcomed with open arms. By all these dreadful people. These cretins, these merchants, these sultans of dry goods and dairy. We've triumphed in Lilliput! Who'd have thought it possible even a week ago?

MILLY. Your fortunes have reversed in reverse.

HOMER.   Exactly! Our fortunes have reversed in reverse. *(Another piece starts playing.)* Oh, this one is lovely.

Oh, I remember this one. *(Milly starts to dress more completely.)*

LANG. Do you remember it from — where do you remember it?

HOMER. Long ago.

LANG. Cathay!

HOMER. *(Starts dancing.)* Yes, Cathay!

MILLY. Oh, have you been to China! I went as a girl, a young girl —

HOMER. *(Dances twice as fast as music.)* Yes!

MILLY. It was so lovely, I thought — so brutal —

HOMER. Yes — I was there — dance with me!

MILLY. Really?

HOMER. Yes — dance with me! — Please — I love the whole thing of parlors — and music drifting from nearby rooms — and lighting! —

MILLY. All right. *(She tries to enter his arms; he's going too fast.)*

HOMER. And when I was in China I met a girl —

LANG. Oh, dear —

MILLY. Could you slow down —

HOMER. A lovely young girl —

MILLY. What was her name?

HOMER. Her name?

MILLY. Yes — what — I'm going to have to *lunge* at —

LANG. Cio-Cio-San —

MILLY. *(Throws herself into his arms.)* Cio-Cio-San?

HOMER. Yes.

MILLY. That's sounds familiar.

HOMER. We *were* familiar.

MILLY. Are you sure that's a *Chi*nese name?

LANG. Cathay! Cathay!

MILLY. Are you dancing a polka? Because they're playing a waltz.

HOMER. And she loved me absolutely.

MILLY. That's nice.

HOMER. Horribly, terribly, and we would "dance" —

MILLY. That's —

HOMER. But I seduced and abandoned her —

MILLY. Oh, dear.

HOMER. I was handsome, then. And Caucasian. And I could do that sort of thing. It was acceptable.

MILLY. Why are you dancing so fast?

HOMER. She had my child — I left her — sometimes I wonder what became of her — I'll have to go back someday — and see —

MILLY. Wait a second. (*They stop dancing.*)

HOMER. ... What?

MILLY. That story —

HOMER. ... Yes?

MILLY. It's from a play! I saw that story in a play! Last season.

HOMER. You might have seen something like it on the stage —

MILLY. It! It! It! The very thing — the whole thing — only she was *Nip*ponese — not *Chi*nese —

HOMER. There might have been something along those lines on the Broadway stage — such things have been known to —

MILLY. The Thing Itself! The Thing Itself!

HOMER. It's — possible —

MILLY. It was in a play. It was something contrived by a playwright —

HOMER. Well, where do you think he got the idea?

MILLY. I — well — he contrived it —

HOMER. Out of what?

MILLY. His — well — his imagination!

HOMER. His *imagination!* We're talking about a *play*wright! Playwrights don't have imaginations — they're drunken illiterates, every last one of — look: Here's what happened — I *met* this man one day —

MILLY. Where?

HOMER. Where?

MILLY. Yes, where?

HOMER. At ... (*To Lang.*) Help me.

28

LANG. An oyster bar.

HOMER. Yes! At an oyster bar. And I was feeling a bit maudlin. And I began to tell him my story —

MILLY. So then, that play was drawn from life?

HOMER. From my life, yes —

MILLY. I saw it; it didn't *seem* drawn from life —

HOMER. That's no concern of mine; that's failure of craft —

MILLY. Although the scenery did — Lord, that was realistic! Do you know they employed actual termites to get an authentically termite-eaten look? Except they had to keep rebuilding because the walls kept falling on the actors' heads.

HOMER. Well, it was my story.

MILLY. I don't believe it.

HOMER. Then you're an imbecile —

MILLY. I don't be —

HOMER. I was paid for it!

MILLY. Paid for it?

HOMER. Five dollars. Right then. He said, Young Man, let me *have* that story — I'm a drunken and illiterate playwright and *that* story is the freshest thing I've —

MILLY. What a lot of —

HOMER. And he gave me five dollars on the spot.

LANG. On the spot?

HOMER. On the spot!

MILLY. I bet.

HOMER. You still don't believe me?

MILLY. No.

HOMER. *(Takes out billfold.)* Well ... *(Throws five-dollar bill on table.)* What* do you *say* to *that*?

LANG. Lord! Then it must all be true!

HOMER. I think I'm due an apology —

MILLY. I think —

HOMER. I think I'm due a *formal* apology —

MILLY. I think not — I think —

HOMER. Well, then, stop smoking my cigar!

MILLY. You wouldn't give me one —

HOMER. In that case — stop — oh! There must be *some*thing I can take away from you!

MILLY. There isn't.

HOMER. There must be.

MILLY. That's —

HOMER. There *must* be —

MILLY. No. That's the fact about me. *(Beat. Lang storms up, lunges at the piano.)*

LANG. THIS IS BARBARIC!

MILLY. What is?

LANG. This chaos they're calling music! *(He plays the same piece the quartet is playing but at half tempo.)*

HOMER. Oh, that's much better. *(He rises, once again dances at double the quartet tempo.)*

MILLY. I love dance parties! *(She rises. Dances to the quartet.)*

HOMER. Yes! I remember them from long ago! I MUST SEE TO OUR GUESTS! *(He swirls off through the double doors. Milly stops dancing. Lang looks up, stops playing, sits there. Pause.)*

MILLY. Tell me exactly what you're thinking.

LANG. All girls ask that question.

MILLY. We do.

LANG. It's a preposterous question.

MILLY. Answer it anyway.

LANG. I'm thinking: I wish I didn't have so many senses.

MILLY. So many — ?

LANG. Five. Five is far too many. I wish I could lose one.

MILLY. What else?

LANG. Oh. *(Beat.)* That I had a minute in college when … it seemed …

MILLY. Seemed — ?

LANG. Oh. *(Beat.)* This one … evening. That is to say I *woke* … this one evening and wandered through the suite of rooms I shared with three other men. I was phantom-y — I have acute night vision and — was lighter then — and was — I think — invisible to them — and I visited their — rooms — by which I mean their *bed* chambers — like — less than a breeze — and was not noticed — and — one of the men was — pleasuring himself — with two hands — Lord! That was impressive — and twisting his head into his pillow — and crying out — his mother's name — which was really — and the second of them was — muttering obscenities softly into the dark — and the other — slept — just — slept — breath in, breath out — and that seemed — oddest of all — AND FOR THAT MOMENT — the year that followed — I ... thought that I wasn't ... that I might ... I ... paid attention at football games.

MILLY. This story is about football games?

LANG. Yes — deeply, deeply — about football games.

MILLY. Would you like to take me to a football game? *(Pause.)*

LANG. *(Softly, staring at the keyboard.)* Well, yes, I suppose I would ...

MILLY. Remember this night. Always remember this night.

LANG. I don't have a choice.

MILLY. Always remember this night. We danced. And I showed myself to you naked.

HOMER. *(Appearing at doorway.)* And it's the first really traditional Christmas we've had in years!

Scene 4

Afternoon. Homer and Milly.

HOMER. Welcome, Miss Ashmore, welcome, welcome, once again, to our home.

MILLY. Where is your brother?

HOMER. No, don't worry, it's just us. May I pour you some tea?

MILLY. I want *nothing*.

HOMER. *(Pours her tea.)* All right. You don't have to get huffy about —

MILLY. Where could he have possibly gone without you?

HOMER. An afternoon recital for ladies ... in the *drawing* room of a *lady* —

MILLY. How did you persuade him to do that?

HOMER. I explained to him our finances — the condition of our finances — sugar?

MILLY. No.

HOMER. *(Drops four lumps into the cup.)* I explained to him that the money they were offering was awfully good — I *reasoned* with him, I made him *see* that —

MILLY. How did you get him to go?

HOMER. I hit him *(Beat.)*

MILLY. No. Really.

HOMER. Well, you have to.

MILLY. No. Really.

HOMER. Well, it's Langley —

MILLY. You didn't hit him —

HOMER. He responds beautifully to physical violence — he always has — he becomes an angel of docility. *(Pause.)*

MILLY. That sort of thing doesn't happen here.

HOMER. Doesn't it?

MILLY. You know, Mr. — Homer, I have been trying in these last weeks to figure you out — to sift and winnow through your behavior to me — its violent, even perverse swings — and after careful consideration, I have come to the conclusion that you are extremely hard to read.

HOMER. I shouldn't be — I'm an open book — well, no, I'm more like an open *stack*, really — *Madame Bovary, c'est moi* — and also everybody else in the damn library —

MILLY. You know, I'm not untrained in psychology — and —

HOMER. I *know* this about you — you are utterly *à la mode* — that's your ferocious attraction —

MILLY. What do you think of me, really? What do you think is the relationship among the three of us? How would you put it into words? How would you characterize it?

HOMER. I would say … You're a silly little rich trollop who likes to tease our cocks.

MILLY. Mr. Collyer!

HOMER. Okay, let me try another one:

You are … the spirit of the avant-garde incarnate … a quester after the new; it is by the efforts of you and your likes that the fallen, fractured, machine-wrecked world will once again be made whole.

MILLY. … That's better.

HOMER. I don't know. I think before I was closer to the mark.

MILLY. I can leave —

HOMER. But you won't. Oh listen: You're our *enzyme*. In your presence, reactions take place.

MILLY. Why did you ask me here today?

HOMER. I want to know your intentions toward my brother. *(Pause. She laughs.)* No, no, no. Answer.

MILLY. How can I answer that? Intentions are had *toward* women not *by* them.

HOMER. In this case, we'll have to make an exception.

MILLY. It's not possible —

HOMER. It simply has to be; you'll have to propose to him —

MILLY. First of all, the presumption of you to assume I'm in any way interest —

HOMER. Oh, don't fake —

MILLY. — and even if I were —

HOMER. Is there under all that — persiflage — a hard little throbbing little nugget of convention that really runs you? *(Beat.)*

MILLY. Will I have to sink to my knee?

HOMER. Save that for after the wedding.

MILLY. You're mad —

HOMER. Well, how *else* is it going to happen? Do you expect me to start him in your direction, in some way?

MILLY. Well, maybe I do. *(Beat.)*

HOMER. Huh. I suppose I could *hit* him.

MILLY. Flattering.

HOMER. Oh, it isn't you — it's anything — anything — you can't get him to — that he *washes* regularly is only due to me — I am his — prime mover! — that's —

MILLY. Then — does this mean — you *want* him to marry me?

HOMER. I want the two of you to become engaged.

MILLY. And to marry?

HOMER. Oh no — I'll scuttle that.

MILLY. You'll —

HOMER. Or *fail* to —

MILLY. Which?

HOMER. There's no telling — that's the marvelous part!

MILLY. Then — are we — allies, antagonists — what —

HOMER. Antagonists, I hope — *(Sincerely like an offer of friend-ship.)* I *want* us to be antagonists —

MILLY. Do you hate me, Homer?

HOMER. Not at all.

MILLY. Then why do you act as though you do?

HOMER. Because it makes for a better scene! *(Beat.)*

Oh — look — you excite me — you — ex*cite* me —

MILLY. I know —

HOMER. I am my brother's accountant — do you know? I am: that. *(Beat.)*

I was — when I was — a child — my mother — oh let me start with her:

My mother was a woman of taste.

MILLY. *(Satisfied smile.)* I knew your mother would come into this.

HOMER. If you only knew — the epic saga of my Aunt Prudy's cheap lacquered vase — the infamy of its entry into our house — the diatribes my mother launched against it on a daily basis — and the way she managed — accidentally and in full view of my aunt — to sweep it off its pedestal and smash it into a thousand pieces!

MILLY. So?

HOMER. So?

Well.

I'm not sure ...

That story has always seemed to have a point.

MILLY. "I am my brother's accountant."

HOMER. Yes!

When I was quite young, my mother said to me, "Homer, you are *for* your brother."

Can you imagine?

It was a kind of manifesto for my life; she was not a casual woman, there was an aura of fatality about the way she'd pour the *coffee* — so when she said — and I still so young — "You are *for* your brother" — I knew at once that my life would be devoted to dodging this proposition — because you see — I wanted my own life.

MILLY. Of course.

HOMER. And had it ...

I *do* have — I mean, the *past* ... is *real* ... it doesn't seem so, but it is. It is *true*.

MILLY. I know. I am the ruin of that truth. *(Beat.)*

HOMER. I'm sorry.

MILLY. That's all right. I'm better ... since Vienna ... *(Beat.)* Tell me: How did you get from there to here? How did you end up tending to him, after you'd made your escape?

HOMER. Oh. Well. Fraternal love is a powerful —

MILLY. No, really.

HOMER. He was spending all our money.

MILLY. I *knew* it was money!

HOMER. All our property is held jointly, and it was made known to me that he was squandering it — and I came and took over. *(Pause.)* In addition, fraternal love is a powerful —

MILLY. How *much* money is there?

HOMER. Less and less.

MILLY. Are you in danger of losing everything?

HOMER. Oh, I hope so!

MILLY. Homer.

HOMER. I don't care what happens as long as something does. My brother's life is ... one of ... piecemeal intensities; I watch him.

Some nights — weeknights — I watch him, right around seven P.M. — that poignant, Booth Tarkington hour when people come home. Do you know, sometimes he cries? I can see him *weeping* for it — and I think as long as this still happens, then life is possible. But opportunity passes. I have forgotten how I got from there to here. *(Beat.)*

MILLY. Then I would be the mistress of this house.

HOMER. Yes, sure, fine.

MILLY. I would be in charge of the servants —

HOMER. We don't have servants; every two weeks an old blind woman comes in to spit on the dust —

MILLY. There will *be* servants —

HOMER. We can't keep them.

MILLY. With me here, that won't be a problem. I'll be in charge.

HOMER. Yes, fine.

MILLY. Everything will have to change.

HOMER. "Change"! The most thrilling of all words!

35

MILLY. Now about my money —

HOMER. And there's the second most thrilling —

MILLY. It would have to remain my money. I mean, the marriage contract would have to be accompanied by another, rather more realistic document that my lawyers will arrange. So that in the event of anything at all happening, my property would never be imperiled.

HOMER. You do *love* my brother?

MILLY. Passionately, romantically. I'll call on my lawyer tonight.

HOMER. Fine — I love lawyers — I am one!

You won't...?

MILLY. Finish.

HOMER. — love him too much, will you? Or understand him too completely and let him know it? That wouldn't play well.

MILLY. I understand him implicitly. He is an artist, therefore turbulent, strange, possessed by passions unknown to the common run of people. He needs to be cosseted, indulged, and surreptitiously held in check.

HOMER. Oh, good! Nothing to worry about.

MILLY. *(To herself.)* Marriage to him will be a great spite to my family. *(Beat.)* Well. What a lovely visit this has been!

HOMER. So much accomplished.

MILLY. Yes. *(Lang enters, ashen-faced and wobbly.)*

LANG. Homer — !

HOMER. Lang —

LANG. I can't — I can't —

HOMER. What is it?

LANG. Don't make me do that again — don't make me do that again — don't make me do that again — don't make me —

HOMER. What happened?

LANG. I can't tell you that — I can't tell you that — you *know* it's too much to tell — *(Homer is holding him now, propping him up.)* Please don't make me do it again.

HOMER. No, I won't — no — never — no I won't —

LANG. Hello, Milly.

MILLY. Hello, Lang.

LANG. Why is she here?

HOMER. Oh. We were making some plans?

LANG. Plans!? Do they include me?
HOMER. Only to a negligible degree. Listen, why don't you go up now? Have a bath. I'll bring you something on a tray.
LANG. Yes. Yes, all right. *(Homer helps him out of the room. Left unsupported, he walks, wobbly, off.)*
MILLY. Sweet to watch you walk him like that.
HOMER. Fraternal love is a powerful thing.
MILLY. I must to my lawyer, before it's too late.
HOMER. Yes. What time is it anyway?
MILLY. *(Consults her watch.)* Almost seven.
HOMER. Seven.
MILLY. Yes.
HOMER. Seven P.M.
MILLY. Yes.
HOMER. And I'm in it! I'm in it!

Scene 5

Morning. Lang sits alone in morning coat and top hat. Homer enters.

HOMER. The musicians are getting antsy.
LANG. Oh.
HOMER. They seem to have a subsequent engagement and would like to get underway — is there anything you would like to tell them? Any advice or —
LANG. Are they going to play?
HOMER. Well, of course.
LANG. Are they, in *fact, plan*ning to play?
HOMER. That would complete the bargain, yes.
LANG. They're going to play the Wedding Knell. *(Beat.)*
HOMER. Technically, it's a *march.*
LANG. That's my least favorite kind of music.
HOMER. Be that as it may —

LANG. I abominate marches. If I had the money — and the wherewithal — to order an assassination — my target would be John Philip Sousa —

HOMER. Lang —

LANG. John Philip Sousa — I would eradicate John Philip Sousa — if I were known — because it seems everyone must be known for something — as the man who killed John Philip Sousa, it would be *fine.*

HOMER. Let me look at you.

LANG. Why?

HOMER. I'm sure something on your person needs fixing. *(Looks.)* Yes. *(Fiddles with his tie.)* Did you bathe today?

LANG. I did.

HOMER. Proud of you.

LANG. You're choking me.

HOMER. That's how you know it's fitting —

LANG. Homer —

HOMER. Yes?

LANG. Will things — start to — *happen,* now? — I mean —

HOMER. You have nothing to worry about. *(Milly enters in wedding gown with a vast train.)*

MILLY. I think we may have Nyack! *(She exits.)*

LANG. What was that?

HOMER. Your bride.

LANG. What was she saying about Nyack?

HOMER. I don't know.

LANG. How do you — how does one *have* Nyack? I don't understand.

HOMER. I don't know.

LANG. Then what *good* are you?

HOMER. I'm —

LANG. What good are you?

HOMER. Lang —

LANG. You know I count on you for spurious explanations of enigmatic conditions; what *good* are you if you fail even at *that?* *(Milly pops back in.)*

MILLY. Or, if not, Dobbs Ferry! *(She pops out.)*

HOMER. That's bad luck.

38

To see your bride before the wedding.

LANG. I didn't look.

HOMER. Are you sure?

LANG. Why would I look? She's not interesting.

HOMER. ... Good.

LANG. ... What a moron you are.

HOMER. Why?

LANG. I don't know — I don't know — God knows it doesn't run in the family —

HOMER. You're being vehement —

LANG. Your superstitions — and your — enchantment with irony — and your terrible, terrible taste — what a moron, what a moron!

HOMER. This is *nerves* ...

LANG. Why am I — forced — to be in cahoots — with such a sentimental — dunce? —

HOMER. You're nervous —

LANG. *God!*

HOMER. Nerves, nerves, nerves!

LANG. GOD! *(Beat.)*

HOMER. Nerves. *(Milly enters.)*

MILLY. Or Croton-on-Hudson. *(She starts out.)*

HOMER. HALT! *(She stops.)* What in the hell are you *talking* about?

MILLY. Oh, dear, how funny! I'm negotiating our wedding present.

LANG. We're being given a *town?*

MILLY. Darling, an estate.

LANG. What do you mean?

MILLY. It's self-evident —

LANG. Homer, ask her what she means?

HOMER. What do you mean?

MILLY. An estate! Grounds, houses, horses, fountains — an est*ate.*

LANG. This is our home.

HOMER. This *is* your home.

MILLY. Yes, yes, of course. Now here's the thing: Nyack you see the Hudson year round, where Croton-on-Hudson, you only see the Hudson in winter, when the trees are bare. Dobbs Ferry you never see the Hudson at all, but it's the size of Madison Square

Garden. I think we have our *choice*, you see, because I'm using blackmail.

LANG. Blackmail?

MILLY. In my situation, it's tremendously effective.

LANG. Milly.

MILLY. *(Enters his arms.)* Oh darling, we have a lifetime of extortions before us. Is your hair really going to be doing that *at the* altar?

LANG. … This … is my home.

MILLY. Of *course* it is.

LANG. This … is my … no, you don't understand … this is my *home* —

MILLY. And this will always *be* your home — *our* home. Always. The other place will be just where we *stay*. On days of the week. *(Beat. Lang's mouth opens in a kind of silent scream. Homer goes to him, holds his head.)*

LANG. Homer —

HOMER. Nothing will happen you don't want to happen.

LANG. Homer —

HOMER. I'm *here.*

LANG. Homer —

HOMER. Eternally. Eternally. *(Lang visibly calms down.)* Would you say something to your father for me?

MILLY. Yes, of course, what?

HOMER. "I'll take it in cash, Daddy." *(Beat.)*

MILLY. We'll arrange for *something. (She exits.)*

HOMER. There.

LANG. You *are* a fixer.

HOMER. Yes.

LANG. There is *that* about you.

HOMER. There is.

LANG. Yes. *(Beat.)*

HOMER. You're getting married.

LANG. Yes.

HOMER. In minutes.

LANG. Yes. How long do you expect the ceremony will take?

HOMER. I don't know — half an hour?

LANG. Hm. Then I suppose that will give me plenty of time to spend with my *stamps* —

HOMER. — to spend with —

LANG. — before I fall asleep — I'll need seven or eight hours — it won't go longer than half-an-hour, do you —

HOMER. Lang.

LANG. ... Yes.

HOMER. This is your *wedding* day.

LANG. In your mind I suppose it is —

HOMER. Shouldn't you tell me that you love me? *(Beat.)*

LANG. Why?

HOMER. Because it's an occasion. *(Beat.)*

LANG. So?

HOMER. Just, please ... do. *(Pause.)*

LANG. I love you.

HOMER. Thank you, Lang. And I —

LANG. Yes, you're very right, I must try to remember that. I must make a mental note to tell you from time to time what it is you want to hear so you won't walk out on me and force me to learn to pay the bills by myself.

HOMER. ... Lang —

LANG. Although, I suppose, now, with, Milly ... *(Pause. The quartet starts playing the wedding march.)* A-A-A-A-A-A-A-A-A-A!!!!!!

HOMER. All right — calm down — I'll stop them — ! *(He goes out. Lang goes to the piano, plays the opening notes of the wedding march slowly. After a moment Milly comes in.)*

MILLY. Those idiot musicians — they've leapt their cue! Absolutely no sense of drama ... *(He stops playing, looks at her.)* Oh dear, what a day. This *room* really *is* a mess ...

LANG. I don't think so ...

MILLY. Look at it — it's a *pig*sty! — what if someone were to wander in from the party? Where's the wastepaper basket?

LANG. We don't have a wastepaper basket.

MILLY. What do you mean, you don't have a wastepaper basket? Everybody has —

LANG. I don't believe in waste paper.

MILLY. You — well that's absurd. That's idiotic. You can not believe in God, or something like that, but you *have* to believe in wastepaper. Wastepaper can be empirically proven. Now, where do

41

you collect your trash?

LANG. ... I don't know.

MILLY. Oh! You are in for such a renovation! Well, we're just going to have to kick this stuff under the furniture and hope against *hope* that nobody looks — *(She starts gathering and hiding.)*

LANG. Stop ...

Stop ...

Stop! Not that!

MILLY. What?

LANG. *That!*

MILLY. ... This? This is a ... piece of string! It's come loose from a pull cord —

LANG. Don't manhandle it like that —

MILLY. Manhandle — oh look, look, I don't have time — we have to get married — but our first act as man and wife is going to be to *burn* this little piece of nothing; now, slick down your hair, puff out your chest and *march*, my angel; it's *time.*

LANG. *(Fondles the string.)* I first saw this when I was in my crib —

MILLY. What? That? Oh, please —

LANG. I looked up — and saw it — it was — dazzlingly colored — nothing is ever lost on me, nothing ever leaves — it was the first thing of its kind I'd seen — and though I didn't know about words yet, I wanted desperately to name it —

MILLY. Why not let's call it string and *get on* with this?

LANG. I remember the desperation —

MILLY. Oh, God.

LANG. — and I remember reaching — Mother was breaking the hated vase, which would one day be legend — the nurse came at me as an apron — vast, white, starched — and some sweet, curdled smell entered the room —

MILLY. Langley!

LANG. — there were tears off to the left — a glittering of porcelain below — a spoon with the sweet white was thrust into my mouth — and piano notes played in the next room — and everything was entirely itself, and all at the same time.

MILLY. They're just going to keep playing that monotonous tune until we show up, so I think we should think about showing up.

LANG. So you see —

42

MILLY. I mean Lord! I have never known anyone to wander into parentheses with the zeal that you —
LANG. So you see the thing is —
MILLY. All right, then, I'll go first. Upending all tradition!
LANG. So you see, the thing is, I can't possibly marry you. *(She turns.)* Not possibly. *(Fade. End of act.)*

ACT TWO

Scene 1

Homer sits drinking.

HOMER. *(To no one.)* And what happened next was ... truly remarkable.
    We ...
    And what happened next will startle you.
    There was a ...
    And what happened next was, everyone dashed about in uproarious confusion; tears and cries and ... And what happened next was ...
    Ah! Well, then, you know that part, good ...
    So.
    Ever since. Ah well.
    Diminishment, diminishment, fatigue. I ...
    Do you know, there was a Frenchman, long ago, who wrote a learned treatise about a lemon peel, which ran to several volumes. I might get Lang started on something like that, if it weren't for his near total illiteracy. His hostility to books. And his categorical rejection of categorical thought.
    If not for those small obstacles, we might get ... a second learned treatise on a lemon peel ...
    But, no, he's too involved, anyway, with his *days,* his ambit — haunting the streets, meditating or foraging, bearing back all this exquisite ... décor. Have you ever *seen* such extraor — have you ever seen such and eclec —
    Oh! What I love about our life is its originality, its revolutionary qualities, its improvisatory nature. I *love* that ... about this ...
    I used to love — on bad days — I used to love — on days

when I'd stayed indoors and weltered in my ... freedoms ... I used to love to walk around the block.

Simply that.

It was like coffee the way everything woke up for me, all possible and kindly — the air — fresh or foul, but *there* —

Of course can't do that much anymore, no, no, not much. Not since they started stoning us. Well: *peb*bling us, the neighborhood children, but still: sanctioned by their parents, even encouraged, I'd warrant.

That's unpleasant, you know. To be hit by rocks for no good reason. For no reason at all. Well. They have their reasons, I suppose ... Things come flying through the window. No *sanctum sanctorum* this. Things come flying. The days all have a dingy brown cast to them. I miss ... everything.

But I don't complain. You'll like that about me. I'm cheerful. I'm stoical. I cook. And I try to force a rhythm on the day. Which in the absence of sunlight and sleep is *quite* a job of work. To take a great undifferentiated wash of time and hack it into seasons. Less resourceful men couldn't ...

Less resourceful men wouldn't be able to ...

Less resourceful men. *(A clock tolls seven. Homer shuts his eyes. Later. Homer sets the table for dinner. Lang enters.)*

LANG. Homer!

HOMER. Good evening, Lang.

LANG. I'm back.

HOMER. Yes, I see. I'm *happy* about that.

LANG. It was lovely.

HOMER. What was?

LANG. All of it. The day.

HOMER. Oh, did they miss?

LANG. Yes, um, well, mostly.

HOMER. I'm glad.

LANG. And even when they — hit — I didn't pass out — or get sick —

HOMER. That *was* a good day —

LANG. Yes — did you cook?

HOMER. Yes.

LANG. What?

HOMER. A stew.

LANG. Good — I'm hungry.

HOMER. Well, there's plenty.

LANG. Good, I'm hungry.

HOMER. Well, there's plenty.

LANG. I was in the park.

HOMER. Ah.

LANG. All day ...

HOMER. Mm-hm.

LANG. It was something.

HOMER. Good. Wash your hands.

LANG. Don't you want to hear about it?

HOMER. Not at all. Wash up.

LANG. Homer —

HOMER. Or I won't feed you. I won't feed you if you have dirty hands —

LANG. My hands are clean —

HOMER. Your hands are never clean —

LANG. They *are* — antiseptic —

HOMER. Your hands are filthy as a coal miner's.

LANG. Spotless —

HOMER. People see your hands they think you're Welsh —

LANG. Why won't you listen to me?

HOMER. Because I know the sorts of things you have to say and I don't want to hear them —

LANG. You — think you do —

HOMER. I'm sure all you have to tell me is the story of a leaf or something —

LANG. — Oh.

HOMER. And I don't feel like attending to the story of a leaf, right now, Lang, I simply don't. I don't want to hear about its texture or its striping or its shape or its rare visual appeal or what you thought to call it, I'd rather listen to a narration of some ancient Roman battle, or just sit in stoney silence eating stew, so wash your filthy hands, please, and let's get on with our meal.

LANG. It was an — extraordinary leaf —

HOMER. I have no doubt —

LANG. It was — truly —

HOMER. A *god* among leaves — I'm sure —
LANG. I — thought something before —
HOMER. Oh, I *am* sorry —
LANG. Don't be that way —
HOMER. I'm not being any way —
LANG. Snide — in that way —
HOMER. I'm not — it's simply that I know how keenly you dislike ideas —
LANG. I —
HOMER. — generalities — abstractions —
LANG. I —
HOMER. — anything without an odor — I know because when I read to you —
LANG. Homer —
HOMER. — when I *would* read to you, that is, from Whitman and Thoreau and Emerson, I remember you so deeply approved their trances and deplored their having written them down —
LANG. Nevertheless there are — one or two principles — I mean — *some* things need to be — put into words — creeds or methods — or. *Or.*
HOMER. Ah.
LANG. And it occurred to me —
HOMER. — as you gazed at this leaf —
LANG. I am ignoring your *tone* —
HOMER. Why not?
LANG. It occurred to me that, everything that is … is *fine.*
HOMER. Was this before or after being pelted with rocks?
LANG. After.
HOMER. Well, then, it's earned. *(Inspects his hands.)* Ugh. Wash.
LANG. It's not as if your stew were worth the tribute of clean hands, you know —
HOMER. Nevertheless.
LANG. Lately it's been — viler and viler — I think you put the wrong ingredients in.
HOMER. Nonsense.
LANG. Yes — you pluck the wrong ingredients from the shelf — once I tasted library paste in the goulash — you've become —
HOMER. That's ridiculous —

LANG. — terribly careless — unless —

HOMER. Possibly a cleaning fluid, never library —

LANG. Unless you're trying to do away with me. *(Beat.)*

HOMER. What kind of tree still has its leaves in December?

LANG. What?

HOMER. I say: What kind of tree still has its leaves in December?

LANG. An evergreen, of course.

HOMER. Douglas fir?

LANG. My name for it is —

HOMER. So then what you were studying, so diligently, all the day long, wasn't even really a *leaf* at all, but more a kind of *spindle?*

LANG. My name for it is —

HOMER. Good Lord, you've been staring all day at a needle!

LANG. My name for it is ... *(Homer is dishing out food.)*

HOMER. Well, *what?*

LANG. Oh. I've forgotten.

HOMER. Well, that's fine, then, isn't it? It means you can go back tomorrow and do exactly the same thing.

LANG. Yes.

HOMER. It means you can go back tomorrow and find exactly the same leaf — oh dear, I hope you *tagged* it — you can go back tomorrow and find the same leaf and *stare* at it again, and *name* it, and forget it —

LANG. I'm still young —

HOMER. Sisyphus had the *best* life, didn't he?

LANG. Yes.

HOMER. He got up in the morning, he had something to do — !

LANG. God, this is swill!

Are you out to poison me? *(Beat.)*

HOMER. Try the wine.

LANG. Homer —

HOMER. I was thinking, Lang, just before, just today, while on my *rounds*, you know —

LANG. Homer —

HOMER. Out to the butcher's for the stew meat, to the dry goods store for twine, you know the route I go, daily, dodging rocks —

LANG. Yes —

HOMER. Like marketing in the Crimea —

LANG. Yes —

HOMER. — and I was thinking — oh no, but I don't want to hurt your feelings. *(Beat.)*

LANG. What ... were you thinking?

HOMER. I couldn't.

LANG. You're going to.

HOMER. No, it's not —

LANG. Homer, please —

HOMER. I was thinking, you've become almost ordinary.

LANG. ... I am?

HOMER. Well — I mean — before we thought — didn't we? — with the piano — that little bubble of talent that came and burst — we thought, here may be someone truly *strange* —

LANG. I never —

HOMER. Authentically *weird* — with all your *ways* —

LANG. I never placed — any stock in that —

HOMER. — and for a while, this weirdness seemed, why aren't you eating? —

LANG. Poison.

HOMER. It seemed worthy of sustenance —

LANG. I live my life the way I —

HOMER. — but lately you more and more resemble — *won't* you try the wine? — you more and more resemble —

LANG. Vintage strychnine, is it?

HOMER. — just a garden-variety neurotic —

LANG. Hm.

HOMER. Just like all the other phobics and inverts and para-noiacs and what have you that modern life presents in such daz-zling array — all the frail, frail people with their iron imperatives: Oh, I mustn't sit *here,* I must sit *there;* I can't wash dishes, I'm afraid of *foam;* I couldn't possibly *work,* I have a terror of *energy* — they're everywhere, it seems: the People Who Simply *Can't.* And they have a single thing in common: They always get their own way.

LANG. I'm utterly renouncing you and food!

HOMER. They always get their way. Do you know, I think I'll become a boring neurotic myself — I'm going to develop an imperative! I MUST BE SERVED! There! What do you think?

LANG. Homer —

HOMER. Only who will be *my* servant? *(Silence. With some disgust.)* I'm not out to kill you, you stupid sprat, I'm just an awful cook.

LANG. You didn't used to be.

HOMER. It's what comes from living alone.

LANG. You live with me.

HOMER. Yes. With you. *(Beat.)* And cuspidors, crushed pince-nez, checkbooks from defunct accounts, pieces of a smashed demi-lunette, plumbing parts, rusted roasting pans, baseballs, spoons, pickling spices — *(A lacrosse stick comes hurling through the window.)*

LANG. *(Goes to it delightedly.)* And a lacrosse stick! *(He carries it delicately, with love.)*

HOMER. A lacrosse stick!
  Look at this place! Will you — *look* at this place?

LANG. That's all I ever do.

HOMER. How can anyone care for all this junk?

LANG. How long and lovely it is — all cracked and burnished — and the basket all snarled —

HOMER. Why do you care?

LANG. It's *lovely*, Homer; it's sacred.

HOMER. Sacred! You're an atheist!

LANG. God isn't the source of what's sacred.

HOMER. Then what is?

LANG. Things in themselves.

HOMER. All this junk — I promise you — one day I will toss out all this junk —

LANG. And I'll go, too.

HOMER. Why?

LANG. It's what I love.

HOMER. How?

LANG. Easily.

HOMER. I try to imagine it — in myself — I try to imagine myself — shunning people — and loving duffel —

LANG. How can there be love without duffel?

HOMER. "How can there be ... love without — " ... Only it's not even duffel. Duffel can be gathered up, you can travel with it, you can *take* it *with* you —

50

LANG. It is with me, Homer. All the time. Every scrap.

HOMER. ... No ... I can't do it. It doesn't work on me. I can't make myself resemble you.

LANG. We're not metaphors for one another, Home —

HOMER. You're the only thing there is for me to know — and I'm failing at it — utterly — and I can't bear it —

LANG. Everything that is, is fine.

HOMER. Not for me. *(Beat.)*

LANG. *(A concession.)* You can throw out the newspapers.

HOMER. Langley?

LANG. Yes, Homer?

HOMER. The newspapers are mine!

LANG. You don't even read them anymore.

HOMER. But they're *mine!*

LANG. Useless things with ugly names.

HOMER. *(A litany.) The Times, The World, The Record, The Ledger* —

LANG. Ugh!

HOMER. *The Times ... The World ... The Record ... The Ledger. (Beat.)* I can't bear it!

LANG. *(Mollifying.)* Everything that is, is —

HOMER. Oh, will you shut up with that inane little bromide!

LANG. You just need to relax. You need to calm down.
    This *is* our life.

HOMER. Maybe I *ought* to kill you.

LANG. Well. That will have to be *your* decision. *(From outside, the sound of Christmas carolers.)* Oh! Is it Christmas?

HOMER. ... Yes ...

LANG. I wonder what they're going to throw at us!

HOMER. No ... these don't seem that sort ...

LANG. Oh. Must be strangers.

HOMER. Yes.

LANG. Excruciating singing.

HOMER. Yes. So pretty.

LANG. The seventh boy from the left is flat —

HOMER. It reminds me of —

LANG. A solid eighth-tone flat — it's torture —

HOMER. — nothing. It reminds me of nothing. *(Homer listens,*

wistful. Lang puts his hands over his ears. The carolers finish, move on.)
LANG. That was hell.
HOMER. Lang? I'm getting married. *(Pause.)*
LANG. Ha-ha.
HOMER. No, I mean it.
LANG. Ha.
HOMER. No, I mean it.
LANG. You lie —
HOMER. I'm going to get married ... awfully soon —
LANG. You lie in your very own *house* —
HOMER. You must prepare for it —
LANG. Yes. All right.
HOMER. You must make some attempt to master the minutiae
of your own existence because I'll be too busy —
LANG. — of course —
HOMER. — copulating and so forth — to see to it — that you
don't — reek or starve or —
LANG. Yes, fine —
HOMER. — impale yourself on something *sacred* —
LANG. — yes, of course, Homer —
HOMER. Because in a minute I'll be — blind — and toothless
— and no longer eligible and I can't — pass up the last chance I
may ever have to ... to ... to ...
LANG. I understand. *(He goes back to the lacrosse stick. Pause.)*
HOMER. *(A stifled cry.)* Lang! *(Lang looks at him.)* Please ... read
to me.
LANG. I hate that job.
HOMER. Please.
LANG. Why can't you read to yourself?
HOMER. I'm afraid ... we'll stop talking. I'm afraid, the evening
will go silent ... Please. *(Lang pulls a book off the shelf.)*
LANG. *(Reads.)* "It was utterly wonderful to me to find that I
could go so heartily and headily mad; for you know I had been
priding myself on my peculiar sanity!" *(Tosses book over his shoul-
der. Picks up another book.)* "In recording everything that the
Roman people has experienced in successive wars up to the time
of writing I have followed this plan — that of arranging all the
events described as far as possible in accordance with the actual

52

times and places." *(Picks up another book.)* "To regard all things and principles of things as inconstant modes or fashions has more and more become the tendency of modern thought." *(Again.)* "My purpose is to consider if, in political society, there can be any legitimate and sure principle of government, taking men as they are and laws as they might be." *(Again.)* "If this should be the case with you, you will eternally curse this day, and will curse the day that ever you was born, to see such a season of the pouring out of God's spirit, and will wish that you had died and gone to hell before you had seen it." *(He looks up.)* Is that enough? *(Pause.)*

HOMER. *(Quiet despair.)* Yes.

LANG. Yay! *(He returns to the lacrosse stick.)* Time for this!
Time for everything ...
Homer?

HOMER. ... Yes?

LANG. I love our life. *(Pause.)*

HOMER. Oh.

Scene 2

Middle of the night. The doors to the front hall open. Light streams in from outdoors. Loud slow knocking at the front door. Homer appears, peeks around the stairs.

HOMER. *(Whispers.)* ... Yes? *(More knocking. Slightly louder.)* Yes?

VOICE. Please ...

HOMER. Go away.

VOICE. Please let me in.

HOMER. ... Go away. This is not where you mean to be.

VOICE. Please help me.

HOMER. Ah.
Go away now.

VOICE. Please help me. It's Christmas.

HOMER. Yes. Merry Christmas. Please leave. *(Knocking again.)*

Please don't do that!

VOICE. I should like to come in ...

HOMER. Oh no.

Maybe once upon a time ... *(Knocking.)* Please stop pounding!

VOICE. I will.

Knock-knock.

HOMER. Who's there — oh dear God!

Please ... go. We are in bad enough odor with the neighbors as it is.

VOICE. I'm freezing. I don't mean you any harm.

A corpse in your doorway will look much worse than a wraith in your parlor.

HOMER. ... Oh ... Oh. *(He starts toward door, trips over things, slides a ways.)*

VOICE. Are you all right?

HOMER. I'm ...

No! ...

Yes. I'm fine.

VOICE. Please let me in.

HOMER. Yes, I will. *(He gets up, crosses to door, unlatches it. A woman enters in a hooded cape, ashen, sickly.)* Who are you?

PERSON. The Ghost of Christmas Past, of course.

HOMER. Why have you come here?

PERSON. I've always found this house inviting. *(Beat.)*

HOMER. I don't understand.

PERSON. Is there someplace I can warm my hands?

HOMER. No. We can't go lighting a fire at this hour. Besides they're dangerous these days, it's a house full of kindling, nothing but, so, no, I'm afraid there's no place a person can warm his or her hands at all — *(She shivers.)* Yes. In mine. *(He takes her hands.)*

PERSON. Thank you. It's good to see you again.

HOMER. I'm ... terribly — confused —

You seem to — Who are — *(He stares at her.)*

Milly.

MILLY. Oh. So I've changed *that* much.

HOMER. Milly. What's happened to you?

MILLY. *(Breaking down.)* Everything; everything has happened to me!

Scene 3

A few minutes later. There is *a fire. Milly sits, eating stew.*

MILLY. This is lovely.

HOMER. You're starving.

MILLY. I am, but this is lovely.

HOMER. It doesn't strike you as odd?

MILLY. No. Should it?

HOMER. Well, one pulls anything from the shelf —

MILLY. It's lovely —

HOMER. — without paying attention —

MILLY. Now that you mention it, there is something slightly off —

HOMER. Library paste?

MILLY. No, I *like* the library paste; could it be cinnamon?

HOMER. Yes. Who knows? I may have been reaching for a slim pencil, pulled down the nearest thing — left it for days — threw it in the stew.

MILLY. Lovely. Just lovely. *(She eats, sighs.)* It's getting nice and toasty in here. *(She takes off her hood; her hair is steel gray.)*

HOMER. Oh dear God ...

MILLY. What?

HOMER. There's something on your head.

MILLY. Only my hair.

HOMER. Is that your hair?

MILLY. It's turned, yes ... Please don't stare at —

HOMER. I'm trying to make it out.

MILLY. It's white, that's all. You've seen white hair before.

HOMER. Not on a child.

MILLY. ... I'm not a child anymore.

HOMER. What's happened to you?

MILLY. Not yet, in a moment, not just yet. *(Trying for brightness.)* I've looked — I haven't seen — I've looked on the billboards; Langley doesn't seem to be performing anywhere —

HOMER. ... That's stopped.

MILLY. But why?

HOMER. He's no longer employable. His tempi became too slow.

MILLY. I suppose that's how he heard the music.

HOMER. No. He couldn't bear to let the notes go.

...

Look at the fire. Wouldn't it be lovely if it took the whole room? Wouldn't it be lovely if it spread and spread and took us all?

You can never see things becoming impossible. If only you knew beforehand the forces are ... invisible ... that bring you to a stop, you might be able to prepare ... One day you can't muster the will to cross the room. Open spaces ... impassable ... everywhere ... who saw it coming?

Tell me what happened to you.

Tell me what happened next.

MILLY. Not yet —

HOMER. *Please.* I need to know what happened next. *(Pause.)*

MILLY. It started on the trip back from the wedding-that-never-was. We didn't speak, my mother, my father and I.

All I could think of was fault — and the fault was mine. I had played this part badly. I couldn't endure who I was: my parents' daughter. This rich ninny, this fool.

I took to my bed and would not come out.

Then through the shafts and vents of the house, I heard my parents conspire. Inventing a story to explain away the debacle uptown.

HOMER. *(With barely suppressed eagerness.)* What — what was the story?

MILLY. Illness, they said — the illness of the Collyers — and unspeakable deeds revealed in the nick of time —

HOMER. If only.

MILLY. I lay silent. For days in bed. And soon fell ill. At first I thought it was my mind, my mind attacking my body — that happens sometimes — psychosomatism, it's called — but it wasn't that.

HOMER. What was it? *(Pause.)*

MILLY. I was pregnant, Homer.

HOMER. What! Did something happen I didn't supervise?

MILLY. It wasn't your brother —

HOMER. Did you *cheat?*
MILLY. No.
HOMER. A second Annunciation — ?
MILLY. It happened at home. *(Pause.)*
HOMER. Oh dear God. Dear God.
MILLY. No longer dear to me.
HOMER. What happened ... to the child?
MILLY. It was removed. Thank God.
HOMER. ... I am sorry.
MILLY. Then I started to speak.
HOMER. To speak?
MILLY. In people's houses I took to muttering.
The truth! The truth! This is how things are!
I became the well-dressed madwoman gibbering on the Queen Anne chair.
Until ... my parents ... put me away.
HOMER. Back to Vienna?
MILLY. A public facility.
HOMER. No!
MILLY. For punishment. For warning. A place of bars and strait-jackets and all-night howling.
That's how it ... how my hair ...
And there I almost *did* go mad.
But not quite.
And when I was let out — when it was thought that I was scared enough and scandalized enough to be released without causing harm ... I resumed my story: "My *father* did this — he's not the man you think you know!"
And then I was disowned.
HOMER. This has *twists.*
MILLY. Homer, these things *happ*ened —
HOMER. Yes —
MILLY. To me —
HOMER. Yes —
MILLY. — and were *dread*ful — don't *want* them.
HOMER. No — no — I don't want the *events* — but please give me more of the *story. (Beat.)*
MILLY. My father paid a man — a scurrilous man — to testify

that many years before he had ... lain with my mother. That he, my father, was not my father — this other man — this twisted, terrible man — that's where the madness came from — that's where all the error started.

My mother — disgraced — divorced.

I disowned.

My father free of scandal. Of taint.

A new man.

HOMER. And since then...?

MILLY. I've found the streets to be friendlier than the houses on them. *(Homer sits back, satisfied.)*

HOMER. That tale — what a *corker!* *(He takes her hand.)* I'm so terribly sorry. *(She nods, keeps her hand in his, cries. It builds. He holds her. Lang enters.)*

LANG. Noises ... noises ... nois — what's *happen* — *(Sees the two of them.)* ... No *no* NO! *(And he faints.)*

Scene 4

The next morning. Lang alone, brooding. Homer enters with food on a tray, makes a stumbling path to a table where he lays out settings.

HOMER. Ah, you've awakened!

LANG. Homer...?

HOMER. Last night, I wasn't sure you would.

LANG. Homer...?

HOMER. Suddenly passing out in this place — I wouldn't advise it. All sorts of objects to nick yourself on, to cut and scrape yourself on, to concuss you: weaponry, everywhere, weaponry — sharp edges, blunt weights: Tread carefully.

LANG. Did I pass out?

HOMER. Out! Out! The discovery! — The cry! — then *down* like a plumb line, it was —

LANG. The discovery —

HOMER. — entertaining. Oh. Yes.

LANG. What did I discover?

HOMER. *(To himself but a tease.)* Hmmm.

LANG. ... Homer, I think I saw a ghost last night.

HOMER. A ghost?

LANG. Yes.

HOMER. A *ghost?*

LANG. Yes!

HOMER. You mean an actual, corporeal, flesh-and-blood *spec*ter?

LANG. I thought I saw that girl.

HOMER. Girl ... Girl ... I can't think who you mean ...

LANG. Homer!

HOMER. I can't think *who* —

LANG. From before ...

HOMER. ... From *when* before?

LANG. From the wedding.

HOMER. Oh. *Which* girl from the wedding?

LANG. The bride.

HOMER. Oh! Milly.

LANG. ... Yes.

HOMER. Your affianced.

LANG. *(With some distaste.)* ... Yes.

HOMER. You thought you saw Milly?

LANG. Her ghost.

HOMER. Hmm.

LANG. It was all so sudden.

HOMER. I see.

LANG. She was different ... yet the same. *I don't see how different things can be the same!* But she was. Her hair was ...

HOMER. Ye-e-es?

LANG. ... silvered in the moonlight —

HOMER. *(Smiles to himself.)* Oh in the moonlight —

LANG. Yes — in the moonlight — and she was dead —

HOMER. Well: a *ghost.*

LANG. All her living stuff was gone — bone and blood — but the light transfused her —

HOMER. Oh!

LANG. — exposed her —

HOMER. Ah-huh —

LANG. — separated her particles —

HOMER. Oh dear-dear-dear-dear-*dear*-dear-dear —

LANG. She was herself with *Time* added. *(Pause.) Why did she come?*

HOMER. ... Well, it was a dream *ob*viously.

LANG. Was it a dream?

HOMER. What else? Wash for breakfast.

LANG. I can stay dirty; the breakfast won't mind. It was a dream? Do you promise?

HOMER. Yes.

LANG. Do you swear?

HOMER. Yes!

LANG. Do you promise you swear?

HOMER. I swear on the soul of ... *(Lifts from table.)* this butter-knife: That was only a dream.

LANG. Thank you.
        WHY HAVE YOU SET THREE PLACES?

HOMER. Hmm?

LANG. *Three* places — *three* places —

HOMER. Oh. Have I set three places?

LANG. Yes! *(Beat.)*

HOMER. Well ... you never know when somebody might drop by.

LANG. *Here?*

HOMER. One must always be prepared —

LANG. People don't "drop by" this place, Homer —

HOMER. I read once ... in a book of etiquette — that the successful host — well, hostess, actually — hm. Hm ... Anyway, that the successful host must always have sufficient provender on hand for the odd, unexpected visitor.

LANG. It would have to be an extremely odd visitor in our case.

HOMER. Yes — but you never know, do you? You never know.

LANG. ... Homer —

HOMER. Things might change. *(Beat.)*

LANG. Homer —

HOMER. *(Overlaps.)* Things might be changing as I speak.

LANG. *(A plea.) Homer* —

HOMER. *As I speak.*

60

LANG. Homer?

HOMER. Yes, Lang?

LANG. *Why are you setting places?*

HOMER. Oh, dear.

LANG. We don't *do* that here.

HOMER. Stop whining.

LANG. *What's going on?*

HOMER. Nothing, Lang.

As ever.

LANG. Do you swear?

HOMER. Of *course* I do.

Everything is as it was. *(Milly enters.)*

MILLY. Good Morning.

LANG. *(A scream.)* A-A-A-A-A-A-A-A-A-A-A-A-A! *(He drops like a plumb line, closes his eyes, opens them again.)*

HOMER. Hmmm.

MILLY. That again.

LANG. Oh no. I'm still *here*. I'm still *awake*.

HOMER. Isn't that the trouble: Things are never the same, merely identical. *(To Milly.)* Did you sleep?

MILLY. I did, finally.

LANG. I'm *awake* — it's daylight —

HOMER. Finally?

MILLY. I had to adjust to comfort.

HOMER. That room seemed comfortable to you?

MILLY. It had walls.

HOMER. Oh so you were able to find the walls, were you?

LANG. I'm very unhappy!

MILLY. Yes —

HOMER. *In*teresting —

MILLY. I couldn't *see* them, mind you —

HOMER. Oh no, no —

MILLY. But I felt them — I mean to say, I could de*duce* their presence —

HOMER. Oh, yes —

LANG. I'm very *very* unhappy —

MILLY. And a ceiling, too!

HOMER. Yes, yes — we pride ourselves on supplying all the

61

amenities —

MILLY. *(Looks around.)* I should say! It's a veritable bazaar in here — how did you ever acquire such interesting miscellany?

HOMER. This stuff, you mean?

Gifts, mostly. From the neighbors.

LANG. *How* did this *hap*pen?

MILLY. Have you become popular with the neighbors?

HOMER. With the neighbors who have *pitch*ing arms, we are.

MILLY. Ah.

HOMER. Things come winging through the broken glass — bricks and books and things — Lang takes charge of them.

MILLY. In what sense "takes charge."

HOMER. You might well ask.

Yes — objects enter — Lang doesn't reject them — he doesn't burn them or pulp them or return them — he curates them —

MILLY. How nice.

HOMER. Assesses their value — dwells —

LANG. Answer me —

HOMER. I mean that seriously —

LANG. *Answer me* —

HOMER. Others merely have homes — we truly have a *dwelling* place.

LANG. YOU MUST LEAVE NOW! *(Pause.)*

HOMER. I think not.

LANG. I de*mand* it.

HOMER. I *counter*mand it.

LANG. This is my *home!*

HOMER. Well, maybe it isn't. *(Beat.)* I *am* after all a lawyer. Maybe I've had you declared incompetent and taken control of your interests.

LANG. You didn't.

HOMER. I *might* have. Having you found incompetent wouldn't exactly be an Herculean feat. I mean: Maybe I have.

LANG. Homer —

HOMER. And if I haven't, maybe I will.

LANG. ... I refuse this!

HOMER. Ah!

LANG. I will not be drawn into your ... grubby ... contingencies —

HOMER. All right. Then sit up straight and eat your breakfast.

LANG. Not while she's here, no! No! No!

HOMER. (Explaining to her.) A tantrum.

LANG. Besides there isn't any.

HOMER. What?

LANG. Breakfast.

HOMER. Where?

LANG. On these plates.

HOMER. Of course there is.

LANG. There isn't.

HOMER. Isn't there?

MILLY. Actually no. (Homer squints at plate.)

HOMER. I'd forget my head if I had my druthers. There are biscuits, I'll fetch them. (He stumbles over stuff on the way to sideboard.)

MILLY. Careful!

HOMER. CAN'T THERE BE A STRAIGHT LINE BETWEEN ONE POINT AND ANOTHER *SOMEWHERE* IN THIS HOUSE?

LANG. There's nothing but straight lines.

MILLY. Are you all right?

LANG. Very very short straight lines.

HOMER. I am … thank you.
        Thank you for asking.

MILLY. Well, of course. (Homer returns gingerly with a plate of biscuits.)

HOMER. I am unused to someone asking.

MILLY. Of course.

LANG. (Slams hands on table.) GET OUT!

HOMER. Pay no attention to him. Have a biscuit instead.

LANG. It's probably poisoned.

HOMER. I can assure you it's not poisoned; it just tastes that way.

MILLY. I don't mind.

LANG. *Why have you come?*

MILLY. Not to accuse you, you needn't worry about that.

LANG. Accuse me? What could you accuse me of?

HOMER. All sorts of things — breach of promise — !

LANG. Breach of *pro*mise — ?

HOMER. It's done in these situations — it's even traditional —

LANG. In bad literature —

HOMER. Well, life is like that sometimes —

LANG. In the books you used to read —

MILLY. Used to?

LANG. *Why have you come?*

MILLY. This is as good a place as any to die. *(Beat.)*

HOMER. Better. Here the difference is so much less marked.

MILLY. An easy passage ... a slide ...

HOMER. You won't be dying.

MILLY. Of course I will.

HOMER. Not soon ... not soon.

MILLY. After everything that's happened ... what else?

HOMER. I'll take care of you.
    You'll stay here. *(Beat.)*

LANG. N-O-O-O-O-O!

HOMER. You'll stay here.
    I'll tend to you.

MILLY. This is no sort of place to convalesce —

HOMER. Then I'll change it — I'll change the place.

LANG. No no no no no.

HOMER. I'll change it for you.

MILLY. And what will I do for you?

HOMER. You'll *be.*
    You'll simply be.

MILLY. That's not enough.

HOMER. And you'll *read* to me!

LANG. *I* do that!

HOMER. Ineptly.

MILLY. Read to you?

HOMER. It's been so long since I've been with a book.

MILLY. Why don't you read them by yourself?

HOMER. I ... long for the sound of another's voice.

MILLY. Homer, are you blind? *(Long pause.)*

HOMER. Yes.

MILLY. Oh my dear ... my dear ...

HOMER. Not entirely, of course ... not yet. Light still, and shapes and sometimes a good deal more. Now. Eventually, there'll be nothing.

MILLY. I'm so sorry.

LANG. You're WHAT?

HOMER. Thank you for noticing.

MILLY. Dear Homer ...

LANG. You're *blind?*

MILLY. *(Realizing.)* "Blind Homer" — oh God!

HOMER. *(Smiles.)* I know — incredibly pat, isn't it? I find that comforting, somehow. Life goes along — happening or... not... chaotic... and then you're all at once "Blind Homer"! — Literature in*sists* on itself —

MILLY. A pattern —

HOMER. An identity —

MILLY. A solace.

HOMER. Yes.

LANG. I AM IN THIS ROOM!

HOMER. And no one seems to care: funny, that.

LANG. Why didn't you *tell* me?

HOMER. I was hoping one day you might figure it out on your own. I thought one day I might become your object of contemplation.

LANG. Homer.

HOMER. *(To Milly.)* We'll build you up.

MILLY. ... Yes. Thank you.

HOMER. And you'll continue, won't you, your researches on the street?

MILLY. If that's what you'd like —

HOMER. Going out and bringing back information —

MILLY. I shall —

HOMER. About what the women are wearing and the plays in the theaters and whether there's an international war or whatever ...

MILLY. We'll take care of each other.

HOMER. *(Sealing it.)* Very good.

MILLY. Do you know what I've often wondered?

HOMER. What?

MILLY. After the wedding that never was ...

HOMER. Yes?

MILLY. The game was called, the guests adjourned — what happened to all that food?

HOMER. It's under here somewhere.

MILLY. I might have to do a bit of straightening up, if you don't mind.

HOMER. Fine with me.

LANG. You can't let a woman in this house —

HOMER. Oh but I can ...

MILLY. And we'll have doctors!

HOMER. All right.

LANG. When women enter, *events* take place. They should have stopped making them after the first try —

HOMER. Idiocy.

LANG. It says so in the Bible!

MILLY. Unless you finally did go broke. Did you finally — ?

HOMER. Oh no, there was never any danger of that.

MILLY. But ... you said ...

HOMER. That was just a way of moving things along.

LANG. Homer, an adult woman cannot come and simply live in this house — it's an affront to all the decencies! *(Pause. They smile at what a bourgeois prig he is.)*

HOMER. Then I'll marry her.

　　　If she'll have me.

MILLY. *(Softly.)* Homer — *(Homer gets down on bended knee.)*

HOMER. Will you marry me, Miss Ashmore?

MILLY. Of course.

LANG. But — *I* was supposed to do that.

HOMER. Too late.

　　　Oh, this will be fun! What did that German say — all history happens twice, first as tragedy, then as farce?

　　　We'll do it *twice* as farce.

LANG. Homer —

HOMER. *Listen, you:* (And very quietly, he is more fierce, more threatening than we've ever heard him. A new tone entirely.) This woman has come to us. She has entered our home. She is the tiny thing that has happened in our lives, our smidgen of plot, and I want more of it, do you understand?

　　　This house is mine, you're just a boarder here. You had your chances, you had your time, that's *over.* (Beat. He straightens up, dusts himself off.) Now. I am going out, into the day, and seeing

66

about our future.

Meanwhile, why doesn't somebody find a broom? *(And with great dignity, he walks out, stumbling badly but defiantly on everything as he goes. A moment.)*
MILLY. We might have a fine little time, we three.
LANG. There are poisons in this house — things you can sprinkle on food —
MILLY. *(Mildly chiding.)* Lang.
LANG. Beware. *(Pause.)*
MILLY. Well … *(And she leaves the room. We see how very weak she is as she goes.)* Well.

Scene 5

Years have passed. More detritus has piled up. Thousands of newspapers. Homer sits alone, blind.

HOMER. *(To no one.)* My brother's a special case.

You — you say to me: "You had an outdoor life once, why not coax him into the world?"

My brother makes an epic of a molecule — what would he do with the world? He must stay inside and he must be cared for. I'm more ordinary, and so I tend to him.

How *dare* you talk of the world anyway — so easy, so smug with it — no matter.

Whatever you say …

No matter what you say: *Our life is better than yours. (An old clock comes flying through the window.)* Thanks for the contribution! *(Homer cackles. Homer goes silent. Lang enters.)*
LANG. I've had the most wonderful day!
HOMER. Have you, Lang?
LANG. Yes.
HOMER. What did you do?
LANG. I looked at a bud vase.

HOMER. Oh, a bud vase!

LANG. In the parlor window —

HOMER. Upstairs —

LANG. Yes, the upstairs parlor —

HOMER. In that niche —

LANG. Yes, in the niche — the day was so fine, so bright —

HOMER. Ah.

LANG. I chronicled it —

HOMER. Chronicled, really? In any particular order?

LANG. The history of sunlight through clear glass!

HOMER. And did you write it down?

LANG. I noted every permutation of light. I named shades that have been overlooked by the conventional spectrum. Do you like "dullish apricot"? Or how about "twilight raiment"?

HOMER. Fancy.

LANG. I went wild with the names, Homer —

HOMER. Evidently —

LANG. I was Adam before the inconvenience of Eve! *(Beat.)*

HOMER. Ah. *(Silence. There's a desperation under this now, something resigned, withdrawn, about Homer: a terrible lack of energy that is answered in Lang by unspoken anxiety.)*

LANG. *(Feebly.)* And what did you do? *(Silence.)* Shall we have our walk?

HOMER. I don't feel like it today —

LANG. I'll take your arm —

HOMER. Even so —

LANG. I'll pilot you —

HOMER. No —

LANG. I'll try not to bump you into things —

HOMER. No, thank you.

Thank you very much. *(Beat.)*

LANG. I won't narrate —

HOMER. Even so —

LANG. I won't draw you into culs-de-sac and pick up, say, that teakwood pillbox and tell you, for example that its dimensions are three inches by two inches by three inches and that it's of teak which is a wood deeper-toned than cherry but lighter than mahogany —

HOMER. Lang —

LANG. — and of medium-rough grain, a grain that rises in near-black striations —

HOMER. Lang —

LANG. — and that holding it lightly in your palm does nearly nothing to affect body temperature —

HOMER. Please stop. *(Beat.)*

LANG. But I haven't finished.

HOMER. Please stop.

LANG. But I haven't finished.

HOMER. Please. *(With visible difficulty, Lang refrains from continuing. Beat.)*

LANG. I really haven't finished, Homer.

HOMER. Even so.

LANG. But I really haven't —

HOMER. All the same. *(Beat. Lang, forlorn, brightens.)*

LANG. Oh, Homer! I completed the rigging!

HOMER. The rigging?

LANG. Yes. Oh, it was wonderful, I worked it out. All this gantrified rigging, all pulleys and trip wires — so if, say, a thief, an intruder, in*trudes* — DOWN it will come on him — I took all these *objects* — there were actually a few spare lying about the house — and got this netting — tons and tons will come down, killing the intruder, so we're safe.

HOMER. Ah.

LANG. *(With some force, a kind of bruised defiance.)* We're *safe.*

HOMER. … Ah. *(Pause.)*

LANG. The bud vase was … a miraculous — ! *(Pause.)* Homer, have I wasted this day?

HOMER. No, Lang, I'm the one who wastes the day. *(Pause.)* Lang —

LANG. No, no, no, I'm going to read to you —

HOMER. I don't want to be read to —

LANG. Yes — the way you love —

HOMER. Not today — not anymore —

LANG. *(Plucking books from shelves.)* Yes — I'll even go in order the way you like —

HOMER. Not today, Lang — not anymore —

LANG. *(Gritted teeth.)* I'm *going* to do this for you — here's a book! "In the beginning, God created" — oh we already know how this one turns out — I'll get something else —

HOMER. Lang, I'm going to die today. *(Pause.)*

LANG. N-O-O-O-O-O-O-O!

HOMER. But I am. I am. No, quiet now.
    You'll need to be taken care of —

LANG. Don't tell me this —

HOMER. I have managed, when you were upstairs on retreat, with a *hairpin*, I think, I managed to make a telephone call. To someone I once knew, when there were people — someone who can arrange for your care — for an attendant — someone who can handle whatever money needs to be handled —

LANG. DO NOT TALK TO ME ABOUT THE TELEPHONE! I *PRO*TESTED THE TELEPHONE!

HOMER. — and whatever *hygiene* needs to be attended to —

LANG. I'M NOT HEARING THIS!

HOMER. I've written down his name and number, right here, but of course I don't know if they can be read —

LANG. Homer —

HOMER. — so why not give it a look, hm?

LANG. If you do this thing —

HOMER. This is not a thing you do —

LANG. I swear to you —

HOMER. This is a thing that's done to you —

LANG. I swear to you, I'll trip the wire — yes! — I'll trip the wire myself and bring down — all this debris upon my head — I promise you — it will be a suicide-by-things — !

HOMER. And then we'll be a story after all. *(Beat.)*
    Now, here is the paper on which I've written —

LANG. *(Covers his ears, paces, stumbles around the place.)* No-no-no-no-no-no-no —

HOMER. — this fellow's name and number — can you read it? *(Lang lunges to the piano.)*

LANG. Homer, I'm going to restart my career!

HOMER. I don't imagine so ...

LANG. I am — I am — you'll have to manage me — to order me about — remember how you — loved to — here, here — *(He starts playing, too fast for the tune to establish itself, feverish.)* My technique hasn't slipped a bit —

HOMER. What is this?

LANG. Not a bit!

HOMER. What are you — *(Lang hums madly along.)* What are you playing?

LANG. Da-da-duh-duh-duh —

HOMER. Is this "The Minute Waltz"?

LANG. Yes!

HOMER. Why are you taking it so fast?

LANG. Making up for lost time! *(And he stops abruptly.)* Oh please don't.

HOMER. It's not my *choice,* Lang.

LANG. Don't do this now.

HOMER. It will always be "now" ...

LANG. You can stop it —

HOMER. It's happening.

　　　All I can do is succumb. *(Outside, carolers sing.)*

LANG. Homer, is it Christmas *again?*

HOMER. It seems so, Lang.

LANG. As it was ... this day ... a year ago ...

HOMER. Yes, Lang.

LANG. *(Agonized.)* There's such a thing as a year ... *(Seized by panic.)*

　　　Oh God — oh God — oh God —

　　　I have to — I need — I need to — there are *things* I need to *do* — rites and celebrations, ceremonies I need — to accomplish — schedules I need to — abide by — observances and — tasks — but what — what are they? Oh, what do people do who live in a row?

　　　Homer!

　　　I have to confess myself!

HOMER. I think that's taking it a little far.

LANG. Yes — yes — I have to confess myself to you if you insist on — I mean, if you're *going* to —

HOMER. All right — all right — yes — all right —

LANG. I have to — expiate my sins —

HOMER. Oh dear, you are going whole hog, aren't you?

71

LANG. You have to ... absolve me of my ... sins —

HOMER. All right, Lang, all right.

LANG. ... That girl ... that girl who came here ... that time ...

HOMER. ... Milly.

LANG. Yes, that woman —
When she died ... like that ...

HOMER. Yes.

LANG. I mean, when she *per*ished that way —

HOMER. ... Yes —

LANG. On the eve of your wedding on the bed with the quilt, the quilt that's made of six-hundred-thirty-six mismatched squares of —

HOMER. *(Moving him along.) Yes*, Lang, yes...?

LANG. ... *I* did it. *(Pause.)*

HOMER. She died of tuberculosis.

LANG. I *wished* for it.

HOMER. *(Gently.)* I know you did.
But she died of tuberculosis.

LANG. No. She died of my wish.
(Anguished.) Even a wish...!
(Beat. Then simply.) It's a mistake to start. *(Beat.)*

HOMER. *(Extends the paper.)* Can you read this?

LANG. *(Takes it, lets it fall unread in a heap.)* ... Yes.

HOMER. And you will call?

LANG. *What will I do?*

HOMER. You'll call.
Someone will take care of you.

LANG. It won't be the same.

HOMER. It will be ex*act*ly the same.
A stranger will tend to you.

LANG. What will I have?

HOMER. You'll have what you've always had.
You'll have your things.

LANG. My...?

HOMER. Your collection.
Your duffel.

LANG. *(Looks around, distant.)* Yes ... But Homer?

HOMER. Yes, Lang?

LANG. What's the use of duffel ... without love? *(Homer turns in Lang's direction. Gradually he smiles. Then he goes very still. After a moment:)* Homer...? *(He draws closer.)* Homer...? *(Closer still. Lang stares at Homer. Then shuts his eyes with two fingers. A moment.)* N-O-O-O-O-O-O-O-O-O-O-O — ! *(He charges a hill of junk, throws himself on it, slides down. Then he rushes to the pulley system that runs the junk trap, reaches for it, can't bring himself to do it. He just stands for a moment, lost. Then, like a mantra:)* Everything that is, is fine; everything that is, is fine; everything that is, is ... *(He lifts his head to look at Homer. Stiltedly, he rises and crosses to him. Circles his body. Then he props Homer up in the chair, arranges him until he takes on the aspect of a statue. Walks back to a chair.)* All right ... all right ... all right ... all right ... *(Lang seats himself across from Homer.)* Just don't move ... *(Lang tilts his head, contemplates his brother.)* Just — please! — don't move ... *(Fade out.)*

End of Play

PROPERTY LIST

Lacrosse stick
Clock
Dictionary (HOMER)
Bottle and glasses (HOMER)
Cigar and lighter or matches (HOMER)
Billfold containing five-dollar bill (HOMER)
Tea service (HOMER)
String (MILLY)
Table settings (HOMER)
Stew (HOMER, MILLY)
Serving spoon (HOMER)
Books (LANG)
Food on a tray (HOMER)
Plate of biscuits (HOMER)
Piece of paper (HOMER)

SOUND EFFECTS

String quartet
String quartet playing the wedding march
Clock tolling
Christmas carolers
Knocking

NEW PLAYS

★ **MONTHS ON END by Craig Pospisil.** In comic scenes, one for each month of the year, we follow the intertwined worlds of a circle of friends and family whose lives are poised between happiness and heartbreak. "...a triumph...these twelve vignettes all form crucial pieces in the eternal puzzle known as human relationships, an area in which the playwright displays an assured knowledge that spans deep sorrow to unbounded happiness." –*Ann Arbor News.* "...rings with emotional truth, humor...[an] endearing contemplation on love...entertaining and satisfying." –*Oakland Press.* [5M, 5W] ISBN: 0-8222-1892-5

★ **GOOD THING by Jessica Goldberg.** Brings us into the households of John and Nancy Roy, forty-something high-school guidance counselors whose marriage has been increasingly on the rocks and Dean and Mary, recent graduates struggling to make their way in life. "...a blend of gritty social drama, poetic humor and unsubtle existential contemplation..." –*Variety.* [3M, 3W] ISBN: 0-8222-1869-0

★ **THE DEAD EYE BOY by Angus MacLachlan.** Having fallen in love at their Narcotics Anonymous meeting, Billy and Shirley-Diane are striving to overcome the past together. But their relationship is complicated by the presence of Sorin, Shirley-Diane's fourteen-year-old son, a damaged reminder of her dark past. "...a grim, insightful portrait of an unmoored family..." –*NY Times.* "MacLachlan's play isn't for the squeamish, but then, tragic stories delivered at such an unrelenting fever pitch rarely are." –*Variety.* [1M, 1W, 1 boy] ISBN: 0-8222-1844-5

★ **[SIC] by Melissa James Gibson.** In adjacent apartments three young, ambitious neighbors come together to discuss, flirt, argue, share their dreams and plan their futures with unequal degrees of deep hopefulness and abject despair. "A work...concerned with the sound and power of language..." –*NY Times.* "...a wonderfully original take on urban friendship and the comedy of manners—a *Design for Living* for our times..." –*NY Observer.* [3M, 2W] ISBN: 0-8222-1872-0

★ **LOOKING FOR NORMAL by Jane Anderson.** Roy and Irma's twenty-five-year marriage is thrown into turmoil when Roy confesses that he is actually a woman trapped in a man's body, forcing the couple to wrestle with the meaning of their marriage and the delicate dynamics of family. "Jane Anderson's bittersweet transgender domestic comedy-drama ...is thoughtful and touching and full of wit and wisdom. A real audience pleaser." –*Hollywood Reporter.* [5M, 4W] ISBN: 0-8222-1857-7

★ **ENDPAPERS by Thomas McCormack.** The regal Joshua Maynard, the old and ailing head of a mid-sized, family-owned book-publishing house in New York City, must name a successor. One faction in the house backs a smart, "pragmatic" manager, the other faction a smart, "sensitive" editor and both factions fear what the other's man could do to this house—and to them. "If Kaufman and Hart had undertaken a comedy about the publishing business, they might have written *Endpapers*...a breathlessly fast, funny, and thoughtful comedy ...keeps you amused, guessing, and often surprised...profound in its empathy for the paradoxes of human nature." –*NY Magazine.* [7M, 4W] ISBN: 0-8222-1908-5

★ **THE PAVILION by Craig Wright.** By turns poetic and comic, romantic and philosophical, this play asks old lovers to face the consequences of difficult choices made long ago. "The script's greatest strength lies in the genuineness of its feeling." –*Houston Chronicle.* "Wright's perceptive, gently witty writing makes this familiar situation fresh and thoroughly involving." –*Philadelphia Inquirer.* [2M, 1W (flexible casting)] ISBN: 0-8222-1898-4

DRAMATISTS PLAY SERVICE, INC.
440 Park Avenue South, New York, NY 10016 212-683-8960 Fax 212-213-1539
postmaster@dramatists.com   www.dramatists.com

NEW PLAYS

★ **BE AGGRESSIVE by Annie Weisman.** Vista Del Sol is paradise, sandy beaches, avocado-lined streets. But for seventeen-year-old cheerleader Laura, everything changes when her mother is killed in a car crash, and she embarks on a journey to the Spirit Institute of the South where she can learn "cheer" with Bible belt intensity. "...filled with lingual gymnastics...stylized rapid-fire dialogue..." –*Variety*. "...a new, exciting, and unique voice in the American theatre..." –*BackStage West*. [1M, 4W, extras] ISBN: 0-8222-1894-1

★ **FOUR by Christopher Shinn.** Four people struggle desperately to connect in this quiet, sophisticated, moving drama. "...smart, broken-hearted...Mr. Shinn has a precocious and forgiving sense of how power shifts in the game of sexual pursuit...He promises to be a playwright to reckon with..." –*NY Times*. "A voice emerges from an American place. It's got humor, sadness and a fresh and touching rhythm that tell of the loneliness and secrets of life...[a] poetic, haunting play." –*NY Post*. [3M, 1W] ISBN: 0-8222-1850-X

★ **WONDER OF THE WORLD by David Lindsay-Abaire.** A madcap picaresque involving Niagara Falls, a lonely tour-boat captain, a pair of bickering private detectives and a husband's dirty little secret. "Exceedingly whimsical and playfully wicked. Winning and genial. A top-drawer production." –*NY Times*. "Full frontal lunacy is on display. A most assuredly fresh and hilarious tragicomedy of marital discord run amok...absolutely hysterical..." –*Variety*. [3M, 4W (doubling)] ISBN: 0-8222-1863-1

★ **QED by Peter Parnell.** Nobel Prize-winning physicist and all-around genius Richard Feynman holds forth with captivating wit and wisdom in this fascinating biographical play that originally starred Alan Alda. "QED is a seductive mix of science, human affections, moral courage, and comic eccentricity. It reflects on, among other things, death, the absence of God, travel to an unexplored country, the pleasures of drumming, and the need to know and understand." –*NY Magazine*. "Its rhythms correspond to the way that people—even geniuses—approach and avoid highly emotional issues, and it portrays Feynman with affection and awe." –*The New Yorker*. [1M, 1W] ISBN: 0-8222-1924-7

★ **UNWRAP YOUR CANDY by Doug Wright.** Alternately chilling and hilarious, this deliciously macabre collection of four bedtime tales for adults is guaranteed to keep you awake for nights on end. "Engaging and intellectually satisfying...a treat to watch." –*NY Times*. "Fiendishly clever. Mordantly funny and chilling. Doug Wright teases, freezes and zaps us." –*Village Voice*. "Four bite-size plays that bite back." –*Variety*. [flexible casting] ISBN: 0-8222-1871-2

★ **FURTHER THAN THE FURTHEST THING by Zinnie Harris.** On a remote island in the middle of the Atlantic secrets are buried. When the outside world comes calling, the islanders find their world blown apart from the inside as well as beyond. "Harris winningly produces an intimate and poetic, as well as political, family saga." –*Independent (London)*. "Harris' enthralling adventure of a play marks a departure from stale, well-furrowed theatrical terrain." –*Evening Standard (London)*. [3M, 2W] ISBN: 0-8222-1874-7

★ **THE DESIGNATED MOURNER by Wallace Shawn.** The story of three people living in a country where what sort of books people like to read and how they choose to amuse themselves becomes both firmly personal and unexpectedly entangled with questions of survival. "This is a playwright who does not just tell you what it is like to be arrested at night by goons or to fall morally apart and become an aimless yet weirdly contented ghost yourself. He has the originality to make you feel it." –*Times (London)*. "A fascinating play with beautiful passages of writing..." –*Variety*. [2M, 1W] ISBN: 0-8222-1848-8

DRAMATISTS PLAY SERVICE, INC.
440 Park Avenue South, New York, NY 10016 212-683-8960 Fax 212-213-1539
postmaster@dramatists.com www.dramatists.com

NEW PLAYS

★ **SHEL'S SHORTS by Shel Silverstein.** Lauded poet, songwriter and author of children's books, the incomparable Shel Silverstein's short plays are deeply infused with the same wicked sense of humor that made him famous. "...[a] childlike honesty and twisted sense of humor." *–Boston Herald.* "...terse dialogue and an absurdity laced with a tang of dread give [*Shel's Shorts*] more than a trace of Samuel Beckett's comic existentialism." *–Boston Phoenix.* [flexible casting] ISBN: 0-8222-1897-6

★ **AN ADULT EVENING OF SHEL SILVERSTEIN by Shel Silverstein.** Welcome to the darkly comic world of Shel Silverstein, a world where nothing is as it seems and where the most innocent conversation can turn menacing in an instant. These ten imaginative plays vary widely in content, but the style is unmistakable. "...[*An Adult Evening*] shows off Silverstein's virtuosic gift for wordplay...[and] sends the audience out...with a clear appreciation of human nature as perverse and laughable." *–NY Times.* [flexible casting] ISBN: 0-8222-1873-9

★ **WHERE'S MY MONEY? by John Patrick Shanley.** A caustic and sardonic vivisection of the institution of marriage, laced with the author's inimitable razor-sharp wit. "...Shanley's gift for acid-laced one-liners and emotionally tumescent exchanges is certainly potent..." *–Variety.* "...lively, smart, occasionally scary and rich in reverse wisdom." *–NY Times.* [3M, 3W] ISBN: 0-8222-1865-8

★ **A FEW STOUT INDIVIDUALS by John Guare.** A wonderfully screwy comedy-drama that figures Ulysses S. Grant in the throes of writing his memoirs, surrounded by a cast of fantastical characters, including the Emperor and Empress of Japan, the opera star Adelina Patti and Mark Twain. "Guare's smarts, passion and creativity skyrocket to awe-some heights..." *–Star Ledger.* "...precisely the kind of good new play that you might call an everyday miracle...every minute of it is fresh and newly alive..." *–Village Voice.* [10M, 3W] ISBN: 0-8222-1907-7

★ **BREATH, BOOM by Kia Corthron.** A look at fourteen years in the life of Prix, a Bronx native, from her ruthless girl-gang leadership at sixteen through her coming to matu-rity at thirty. "...vivid world, believable and eye-opening, a place worthy of a dramatic visit, where no one would want to live but many have to." *–NY Times.* "...rich with humor, terse vernacular strength and gritty detail..." *–Variety.* [1M, 9W] ISBN: 0-8222-1849-6

★ **THE LATE HENRY MOSS by Sam Shepard.** Two antagonistic brothers, Ray and Earl, are brought together after their father, Henry Moss, is found dead in his seedy New Mexico home in this classic Shepard tale. "...His singular gift has been for building mysteries out of the ordinary ingredients of American family life..." *–NY Times.* "...rich moments ...Shepard finds gold." *–LA Times.* [7M, 1W] ISBN: 0-8222-1858-5

★ **THE CARPETBAGGER'S CHILDREN by Horton Foote.** One family's history span-ning from the Civil War to WWII is recounted by three sisters in evocative, intertwining monologues. "...bittersweet music—[a] rhapsody of ambivalence...in its modest, garrulous way...theatrically daring." *–The New Yorker.* [3W] ISBN: 0-8222-1843-7

★ **THE NINA VARIATIONS by Steven Dietz.** In this funny, fierce and heartbreaking homage to *The Seagull*, Dietz puts Chekhov's star-crossed lovers in a room and doesn't let them out. "A perfect little jewel of a play..." *–Shepherdstown Chronicle.* "...a delightful rev-elation of a writer at play; and also an odd, haunting, moving theater piece of lingering beauty." *–Eastside Journal (Seattle).* [1M, 1W (flexible casting)] ISBN: 0-8222-1891-7

DRAMATISTS PLAY SERVICE, INC.
440 Park Avenue South, New York, NY 10016 212-683-8960 Fax 212-213-1539
postmaster@dramatists.com www.dramatists.com